conscious
COPING

—— *How to* ——

Stop Fighting Your Mental Health,
Embrace Your Challenges,
and Learn a New Way to Cope

LAURIE SHARP-PAGE
MS, LPCC-S, CWC

First edition

Editing by Lia Ottaviano

Cover art & Typesetting by Jasmine Hromjak

CONTENTS

Acknowledgments v

PART ONE: You Can Cope with Tough Things 1

  1. The Worthwhile Sting of Rejection 15

  2. Foundations of Conscious Coping 39

PART TWO: A New Way to Cope 63

  3. What is EMBRACE? 75

  4. Engage 79

  5. Monitor 97

  6. Brief (and debrief) 107

  7. Reflect 123

  8. Absorb 159

  9. Capture 205

  10. Endure 211

About the Author 219

For Jason, who taught me to jump in.

ACKNOWLEDGMENTS

It is imperative to acknowledge the many teachers and schools of thought who have guided me along this journey. Conscious Coping and the EMBRACE model would not have been possible without the essential and pioneering work of the many psychotherapists before me. Conscious Coping is grounded first and foremost in existential psychotherapy and pulls from other schools of thought including acceptance and commitment therapy (ACT), cognitive behavioral therapy (CBT), dialectical behavior therapy (DBT), mindfulness, and narrative therapy, as well as various creative expression therapies. I used all these approaches in conjunction to arrive at an interdisciplinary framework for how you learn how to cope most effectively.

Other teachers and schools of thought play a role in the development of the model; in the pages ahead, I will do my best to attribute to each one. In some cases, I draw upon tools and approaches taught to me by other psychotherapists, who themselves acquired these tools via other psychotherapists. In those cases, it is difficult to attribute the exact source. However, I would like to acknowledge the past, present, and future psychotherapists who are out there doing excellent work and helping us grow our field by developing creative and unique tools. These people and their work benefit not just them and their clients and us but the entire human race. All these approaches have brought me more peace in my understanding of myself and how I cope. It is truly an interdisciplinary model woven together by the extraordinary lessons of many teachers.

I must also thank my clients. A bonus of being a psychotherapist is having deep and meaningful relationships with other humans. Although the focus of our time together is not me, they have gifted me with many lessons and insights over the years. Whenever a client thanks me for my work, I take a moment to receive their gratitude before reflecting it back at them. They are the ones that show up and do the hard work of growing, changing, and progressing. Although I am the privileged one who holds space for them to do this work, they are the heroes doing it.

In the pages ahead, I will share some client stories. I would like to take a moment and discuss the considerations I have taken to maintain their confidentiality. When I reference a client's story, I will use the pronoun they. I do so to provide an additional level of confidentiality and ground the inclusivity of these challenges and their presentation in treatment. Additionally, I have blended clients' stories where appropriate and possible to do so. This was done to ensure confidentiality and further reinforce the universal nature of these concepts.

You will also see a few stories about my husband and the lessons he has taught me as well. He has been my partner throughout my journey to learning about myself and there is no telling the full story of my development without including him and our journey together.

Finally, I must acknowledge my family and friends who have supported me and the completion of this work. They have been my greatest teachers and champions. You have all cheered me on along the way, for which I am deeply grateful. It is a privilege to have a support system as caring, insightful, and rowdy as you. *I love you all.*

PART 1

You Can Cope with Tough Things

I have something important to share with you. *You can cope with tough things.*

I know this because I have learned that *I can cope with tough things.*

When it comes to your mental health, you may be wondering (or have wondered) "What is wrong with me?" or "Am I crazy?" or even "Is it just me?" As a psychotherapist, these are all questions I have heard from many people over the years. I have been asked these questions by a spectrum of people, which leads me to believe that most, if not all of us, ask them. Even so, my answers to these three questions have never wavered.

You are an imperfect human; nothing is wrong with you. You aren't crazy. We are all challenged by our mental health. Our mental health challenges us in ways that are unique to us and shift across our developmental lifespan. And finally, most important, it is not just you; it *is all of us.* That's right, I said it; in fact, let me reiterate: **WE ALL HAVE MENTAL HEALTH CHALLENGES.** It only feels isolating because *we don't talk about it.* We don't talk about it because we fear something may be wrong with us, that we may very well be crazy, or that it must just be us who is struggling. Sound familiar? Yeah, me too. Remember, I am the professional. I have the language, education, support system, and motivation to live my best mental health life, *and I still struggle.* You likely struggle too, maybe not always, and maybe not to the point that you have a mental health diagnosis or have ever sought mental health treatment, but I see you there, fellow human, and I am giving you permission to admit your challenges. When we acknowledge our challenges, we can stop fighting them, and it is only then that we can learn to cope with them. The purpose of this book is to shine a light on some mental health challenges that you may be experiencing and to encourage you to EMBRACE them, even when you don't think you can cope with them. *Especially when you don't think you can cope with them.*

The worst part of these types of critical questions is that they obscure the most important question: "How will I cope?". The short answer to that question is that you must learn how you cope. You have to figure that part out on your own; no one else can do that for you. The answers are within you, and you must do the work to cultivate them.

The long answer is in the next 200 or so pages. It's important to note that you don't have to prescribe to my method, but you must face your mental health and how you cope with it at some point. If you are interested in living a contented, meaningful, and fulfilling life, this is work you will have to do.

Coping is important; it is key to taking care of our mental health. As a culture, we have been avoidant to our mental health and all the consequences of it. It turns out that when you spend your time invalidating your mental health, there isn't much need to develop a more helpful universal language. We've encouraged ineffective coping through our inability to discuss our murky and abstract minds. As a result, we have lost out on a significant amount of meaningful learning, development, and growth.

While one in five of us will meet the criteria for mental health pathology within our lifetimes[1], 100% of us struggle with our mental health. Just because you are not depressed does not mean you do not struggle with sadness or grief. Just because you do not have generalized anxiety disorder does not mean you will not ever struggle with your anxiety. While you may not have experienced a mental health crisis yourself, that does not mean that someone you love hasn't experienced one, which is itself a difficult thing to cope with. Unfortunately, often mental health education is only made available to individuals with pathology. You should not need a diagnosis to access information on how to cope with your mental health, just as you do not need a diagnosis for your struggle with mental health to be valid.

All that being said, I need to be clear that this book's approach is to provide a baseline intervention—one which we all need to undertake. It is not intended to devalue or replace the role of pathology and associated interventions within mental healthcare. If you are having a mental health crisis or dealing with any type of pathology, *this book will not fix, remove, or change those very real challenges.* You cannot simply cope your way out of depression or schizophrenia. It would be irresponsible and unethical of me not to be clear about that. The goal of this approach is only to change how you view and relate to your mental health and, by doing so, find more intentional and proactive ways to cope. Your mental health may include pathology;

---

1 NIMH, Mental Illness, National Institute of Mental Health (NIMH), accessed December 2, 2021, https://www.nimh.nih.gov/health/statistics/mental-illness.

mine sure does! Or it may not. In my mind, it does not matter if pathology is present or not. Changing your relationship with your mental health and learning how to cope with it is important work for everyone. However, the simplicity of this approach should not be used to minimize the diverse range of mental health challenges that we all face. This book is intended to be a starting point.

As a practicing psychotherapist, people sometimes think I have magic answers or quick fixes; I do not. However, my work as a psychotherapist allows me to be curious about myself and others, and it is through this curiosity that I found my life's work. I am passionate about helping people learn about themselves, their mental health, and how they cope. My goal for this book is to contribute to the greater conversation of mental health by encouraging you, the reader, to get curious about your mental health, specifically how you cope with it. I so appreciate you taking the time to join me on this journey.

It is surprising to see my life take me to a place where I write a book on coping. I'm confident the crowd I ran around with when I was in my early 20s would not believe that someone who coped so messily then would ever be able to help others learn how to cope. They wouldn't be alone in having those thoughts. I've wondered if I, a person who has coped very ineffectively at times, have any right to write a book on coping. The thing is, my career has afforded me a very special purview into the world of mental health. It's not just me, and it's not just you; it's all of us. We all struggle, certainly not to the same degrees, not in the same ways, but all of us, across our lifespans, have mental health challenges.

I have struggled with my mental health throughout my life. My mental health struggles created extra stress and challenges in my life. I've had many seasons when I have coped ineffectively with these things and some when I have coped effectively. When I think back to those messy times that make me cringe, I am astonished by how well I am coping now. It is strange to catch yourself coping well after years of not coping so well—it's like catching yourself in the mirror unexpectedly and liking what you see. An energizing reminder that you have something to feel proud of.

So, what changed? Well, my perspective changed. Slowly, I started to shift into a new way of being. I started doing things for myself that were healthier and more intentional; I started paying attention to how I was coping and strategically coping in ways that got me closer to what I wanted out of life. I learned to feel it all instead of hiding from it all. Instead of ignoring my boundaries and numbing the anger I felt when people violated them, I started asserting and maintaining my boundaries. I learned to cope with and, by default, increase my tolerance to guilt. I learned how not to let uncomfortable feelings deter me. I learned how to be simultaneously happy AND sad, and just as importantly, I learned to accept that these opposing truths can collide. I practiced radical acceptance of all the things within me, over which I have no control. It has been a grind, but here I am coping effectively *and* writing a book about it.

I have been grappling with this project for a long time, primarily because I did not have the language to accurately express what I was experiencing, let alone what I wanted to accomplish with this book. In terms of mental health, language is the most valuable tool we have. Yet, woefully, most of us are not well equipped with verbiage to help ourselves accurately and effectively explain our emotional experiences to ourselves or others. Let alone how you cope with them.

Another challenge in authoring this book was that so much of our focus on mental health has been pathology. A big part of the reason for this is that if there is something wrong or defective in our mental health, then that means there must be *a fix for it*. And to be blunt, there is a lot of money to be made in finding quick fixes for hard things in life. People have long looked to find something to fix within themselves when the answer has never been to fix. This is where acceptance comes in. If we can learn to embrace our internal and external challenges and learn how to cope with them, a fix becomes unnecessary. It's an out from the never-ending fight with your mental health; you don't have to be defined by your challenges if you learn how to cope with them. The deal is that this is ongoing, challenging work in which you must invest. This book gives you a road map for this work. It acts as a flexible guide, one you can shift, mold, or adapt in any way that works for you.

It is worth noting here that I am writing this at a time when we know more about mental health than ever, but we still know so little. Presently, we are in what I assume to be the early days in developing knowledge about mental health and its associated care. There is still so much to learn. There may be a time in which the message of my book becomes obsolete because we understand the fundamentals of mental health differently. I am at peace with that outcome if it comes, but in the meantime, we must do the hard work of taking care of our mental health and learning how to cope effectively.

It is time to take a different approach to our mental health and view it as a sacred part of human nature. One that is honored, not demeaned. The truth is that in our contemporary culture, you wouldn't necessarily think that feeling your feelings, taking care of your mental health, and consciously coping with all the challenge, chaos, and uncertainty the universe provides would be a radical thing, *but it is*. It takes courage, intention, and energy to do these things, and the act of doing so should be applauded, not ridiculed.

We must shift this toxic avoidance enabled by our perfectionist myths. We need a new, more compassionate approach to taking care of and gauging our mental health. A framework that is rigid enough to support us AND flexible enough to adapt to all the varied challenges we encounter. One that makes space for the deeply personal nature of this work. And, most important, a model that is grounded in the actual value of taking care of your mental health and provides an accessible and concrete way to do so. This book intends to present a thoughtful and innovative model to meet this need. EMBRACE is my best guess, and I welcome and encourage your modifications of it. After all, you are the ultimate expert on yourself, and I look forward to hearing how you consciously cope.

Since we are at the starting point of this journey together, let us take a moment and screen our current coping. I've developed the questionnaire below to help prompt you to think about and gauge your coping in an accessible way. This tool is meant for informational purposes. It is intended for you to see where you are now so that you can reflect on where you are at the end of this journey.

	Completely disagree	Somewhat disagree	Unsure	Somewhat Agree	Completely Agree
I feel confident in my ability to cope with current events	1	2	0	3	4
I feel confident in my ability to cope with future events	1	2	0	3	4
I have coped effectively with ANGER in the past	1	2	0	3	4
I have coped effectively with ANXIETY in the past	1	2	0	3	4
I have coped effectively with EMBARRASSMENT in the past	1	2	0	3	4
I have coped effectively with EXCITEMENT in the past	1	2	0	3	4
I have coped effectively with FEAR in the past	1	2	0	3	4
I have coped effectively with GREIF in the past	1	2	0	3	4
I have coped effectively with HAPPINESS in the past	1	2	0	3	4
I have coped effectively with LOVE in the past	1	2	0	3	4
I have coped effectively with OVERWHELM in the past	1	2	0	3	4
I have coped effectively with REJECTION in the past	1	2	0	3	4
I have coped effectively with SHAME in the past	1	2	0	3	4
I have coped effectively with STRESS in the past	1	2	0	3	4
I know how I am feeling right now	1	2	0	3	4

I am able to manage interpersonal conflict in my professional life	1	2	0	3	4
I am able to manage interpersonal conflict in my personal life	1	2	0	3	4
I have a healthy support system of friends and/or family	1	2	0	3	4
I have access to a diverse range of coping skills	1	2	0	3	4
I know how to use my coping skills effectively	1	2	0	3	4
I have a healthy relationship with myself	1	2	0	3	4
I have the energy to cope effectively	1	2	0	3	4
I can accept feedback from others	1	2	0	3	4
I allow myself to feel all the feels	1	2	0	3	4
I am compassionate with myself	1	2	0	3	4
I am compassionate with others	1	2	0	3	4
I have coped with tough things	1	2	0	3	4

0-15	**Not paying attention**	You may not be coping effectively, or you may not be noticing all the amazing coping you are doing; either way, you need to work on paying more attention to how you cope.
16-40	**Low Morale**	You aren't feeling well equipped or motivated to cope effectively. Something has got you down, and you need to find some way to build back your energy. It's harder to cope effectively when you are depleted
41-75	**Scattered**	You're coping for sure, but are you coping effectively? Your disorganized pattern of coping reactively takes a toll on you. Time to get more intentional on how you cope and care for yourself.
75+	**Focused**	You're coping effectively. Are you taking time to intentionally learn from all the great things you've got going on right now? There may come a time when you're not coping as effectively; what can you learn from what is happening now that will help you in the future?

Were your results surprising to you? What thoughts and situations came to mind as you were completing this screener? What information from this do you think is most vital for you to reflect upon?

Get ready for more reflection. This book is active. It's not just about reading it; it's about living it. I will ask you to think about things differently, try different approaches on for size, challenge yourself to lean into the discomfort, and blindly trust that you know the answers and are well-equipped to find them. So give yourself a gift and give it a go. Let's have some fun and learn a new way to cope.

I only learned how to cope *after* I stopped fighting my mental health. Instead, I started investing my energy in learning to cope with the varied challenges and opportunities my mental health gives me. When I changed how I was engaging with my mental health, a lot of other stuff changed as well. It all changed because I shifted my focus from fixing what was not broken to learning how to accept and support my imperfect mental health. I learned the art of effective coping, and because of that, my relationship with myself changed for the better.

Once my mental health became something that was not good or bad and became something that just was, it made it easier to embrace. I stopped judging and berating myself for my mental health challenges. Instead, I practiced prompting myself to be compassionate with myself and others. I started to see, accept, and even celebrate the complex, flawed human I am. As a result, I have became friends with my mental health. We have a friendly relationship because I have found that being nice works much better than being a jerk to it.

Like any genuine change, this was a process. It was often two steps forward, one step back. But over time, this small change rippled through my life. I was causing positive shifts not only in my relationship with myself but also in my relationships with others. This change also gave me more clarity, more awareness of what I wanted for my life. It gave me more acceptance for what is. Best of all, it gave me more understanding of who I am and how I can support myself better to cope with all the challenges, chaos, and uncertainty that surrounds us. The more I saw how this minor change positively impacted my life, the more I wanted to document my journey to making these changes. I knew there was a great value here, not only in my present understanding of who I am and how I cope but also in helping me build my ability to cope in the future and my confidence in doing so.

This book is a formulization of that process, meant to provide you with a road map to learning how you uniquely cope with all the challenges, chaos, and uncertainty you face. We will delve into the how of this process, but the most important thing for you to know now is this: You can cope with tough things, and building your confidence in your ability to cope with future events is the ultimate act of self-care.

In the pages ahead, you will find a truly interdisciplinary work—a work that has been inspired by varied personal and professional experiences I have had. Ultimately, while I am a psychotherapist first, I believe the work ahead is more philosophical. Therefore, I will be asking you to think differently. I know this is a big ask, but I assure you it will be a good investment.

To make this introduction to a new philosophy of coping as accessible as possible, I have split it into two parts. I want you to think of effective coping as a garden. To grow a diverse and fruitful garden, we must start by tending to our soil. The first part of this book looks at your soil. It walks through the foundational truths that you must accept before embracing conscious coping, as well as the essential elements that must be present for you to cope effectively. Part 1 is the pre-work to Part 2. You must address (not perfect) these things before using the EMBRACE model effectively.

Once you have your soil sorted, you can move on to Part 2, which will teach you how to cope more effectively using the EMBRACE framework. Part 2 is where you will learn how to plant, tend, and harvest from your garden. Ideally, you will use this framework as a tool to get to know yourself better and ultimately better your ability to respond to life's varied challenges. To give you some context for Part 2, I want to go ahead and present the EMBRACE model upon which Part 2 is focused. Listed next to each skill are the essential questions you need to ask yourself when you consciously cope.

E (Engage): What can I do to support myself in this moment of challenge?

M (Monitor): How are my energy levels? Do I feel depleted, energized, up AND down, or unsure?

B (Brief): What do I need to learn about this challenge? Who do I need to consult with? What resources can I utilize to help me learn about this challenge?

R (Reflect): How do I feel about this challenge? What sense can I make of those feelings?

A (Absorb): What do I need to do to consciously cope with this challenge?

C (Capture): What lesson does this challenge teach me? How can I capture these lessons to remind me of what I have learned from this challenge?

E (Endure): How can I use the experience of this challenge to help support me in doing the ongoing work required for conscious coping?

We'll explore these seven skills in greater detail in Part 2. The goal is for you to face your mental health challenges in such a way that propels you forward. Keep in mind that this book is grounded in curiosity, not in absolute fact. I share it with the hope that others will be able to explore, and if they choose, share their versions of effective coping, of which I am certain there are *infinite* examples. Whatever happens, though, I hope this book encourages you to stay curious about yourself, your mental health, and how you cope.

CHAPTER 1

The Worthwhile Sting
of Rejection

The email arrived inconspicuously. I was deep into writing, capturing the early embers of this book, when I heard the familiar beep-bop notifying me of a new email. At the start of the year, I had decided that it was time; it *had been past time* for me to take the next step. To reach deep inside myself and share the messages, the stories, and the wisdom I had accumulated over the past ten years. I had had a stern talk with myself. I had decided that this project was weighing me down. I needed to act towards completing the task at hand; otherwise, I would continue to be haunted by the echoing frustration of unrealized dreams.

After a month of pulling my hair out trying to write something that I felt accurately captured what I wanted to say, I decided on a different approach. I put together a proposal for the local TEDx conference to speak out my ideas in a format that would allow me to test the waters, float my ideas, and see if they would land. The name of my proposed talk was "All the Feels: The Overlooked Data of Feelings." It was a rough precursor to the argument presented in this book, and I had been confident I would be chosen to present.

But there, staring back at me, was a rejection note. *Ouch,* I felt the electric sting of rejection fizzle in my belly. The rejection email from TEDx was simple. "We are sorry to inform you that you were not chosen for callbacks." That is a bummer, I thought; this was not the outcome I wanted. A wave of emotion stirred within me; a small funnel cloud of shame swirled in my neck, threatening to turn into a tornado. I felt like an imposter. I was ashamed for even thinking I had something important enough to say at the regional non-broadcast TEDx event. I wanted to throw up and run away. I do not have time for this! *I huffed to myself.*

I have this thought a lot when I am confronted with a challenge. I knew what it really meant. It was a suggestion that I engage in old ineffective patterns of coping. Look away, nothing to see here. Best if we just avoid whatever feelings are under the surface of this tricky thing. Get a drink, take a nap, eat a cookie, go to TJMaxx, or do whatever you need to do to numb yourself from the reality you are currently being challenged with. I heard the old patterns pulse inside of me, felt their pull, tempting me to disengage. To just pretend the funnel cloud of feelings was not still stirring inside of me.

They nudged me, but they did not pull me in. I had learned that these patterns did not serve me well. I fought my urge, took a breath, and made a different choice. I engaged myself by acknowledging that what I was experiencing was real, valid, and important for me to pay attention to. I took stock of my energy levels, noting that I felt depleted and raw. I wasn't surprised; rejection can really take the wind out of your sails. Even when you are well-versed in coping, rejection is tough.

I drew upon the wisdom of my teachers. I thought of my current therapist, who would remind me that running from the feeling would only elongate my discomfort. And I thought of my dad and his philosophy that mistakes were only opportunities to learn from, and what matters most in life is that you continue to show up and keep progressing. Although I was physically alone, I felt supported by these teachers and their teachings.

As I reflected on my feelings, I cuddled my giant dog Murphy Brown, my (non-certified) emotional support mastiff. She loves to cuddle, and having her immense presence around helps soothe me when I am sitting with something emotionally challenging. Pets are great coping companions. As I sat with the feelings, I invited them in. They are not worth fighting, I thought. I had learned over time that invalidating my feelings was my preferred method of avoidance. I have learned to accept that when it comes to feelings, just because I don't want them doesn't mean they aren't there.

As I noticed my feelings, I started to listen to them, and the funnel cloud lessened. I shone a more conscious light on the debris and felt the feelings shift. I feel disappointed, I said to myself, but as soon as I said it, I realized another emotion was present. I was also irritated that I didn't even make it through the first round. *I feel disappointed and irritated,* I said aloud to myself. I will verbalize my feelings, even if only to myself; it helps cement their realness. When they are not real, it is amazingly easy to invalidate or ignore them.

Usually, I would spend some time listening for what triggered the feeling, but in this case, I already knew what triggered it. Sometimes we do not know what triggers a feeling, which can cause us to feel what Dr. Marc Bracket refers to as a meta-emotion, or a feeling about a feeling such as frustration for not understanding why we feel sad.[2] Sure, emotions can be tricky to deal with, but they should not hold us back from continuing to explore them. The trigger, in this case,

---

2　Marc Brackett, *Permission to Feel: The Power of Emotional Intelligence to Achieve Well-Being and Success* (Celadon Books, 2020).

was rejection. Rejection is hard to cope with; it feels yucky, to say the least, and often causes multiple additional feelings to bubble up.

At this moment, I simply took a deep soothing breath in and listened to my body. We often think of feelings as living abstractly in our minds, but this is more reflective of where our thoughts live. Thoughts are tied closely to feelings, so it is easy to confuse the two, but feelings live more primitively within our bodies, exhibiting themselves as physical sensations. The tricky part is we must learn how to listen for *and* to them. There are many techniques for doing so, and what works best for you is something you will explore within your own process and later in this book.

Curiously, I noticed that my disappointment and irritation existed in two different parts of my body, independent from each other. The disappointment lived deep in my stomach, almost in my bowel. It felt like a heavy pressure, a stone that I could not push. My irritation lived on the top of my head, a burning sensation on my scalp, begging for recognition. It was *very* ticked off to not be seen and validated by the powers that be.

Once I had determined that there were no other feelings present, and I felt like I had gathered the needed information from reflecting, I sat with them for a moment. I could feel the energy drain from me as I engaged these feelings. The feelings themselves were not bad, but they did not feel comfortable, and sitting with them was taking energy from me. I had an urge to disengage, which in this case would have looked like laying on the couch, watching trashy TV, and emotionally eating, but as I was about to do so, I heard myself ask, will that really help?

Sigh. While this behavior would have felt good in the short term, I knew from experience that it would take more from me in the long term. I would most likely fall asleep on the couch, awakening when my husband arrived home a few hours later, groggy and emotion-ally hungover. I would be in a worse space. I reminded myself that I would have to tackle these things, and they were much easier to tackle immediately than down the road. So, I encouraged myself to keep investing my energy in the process of conscious coping. I knew what my feelings were, where they came from, and where they lived within me, but what were they telling me? What coherent sense could I make of them? As soon as I asked myself, I knew they were telling me that my needs were unmet.

This realization wasn't too surprising; I know that often when disappointment or irritation shows up, I have unmet needs. Unmet needs happen; life is full of unmet needs, a truth all of us share. In this case, my unmet need was not receiving the external validation of the importance of my expertise. It was a validation I had hoped for because it would have given me a more concrete path towards digging into this project. Frankly, it would have made this easier in the sense that I would not have to do the challenging work of decid-ing that what I had to say was important without the external seal of approval.

Often when we have unmet needs, we will have a strong reac-tion; sometimes, this reaction is almost automatic. We need to be particularly curious about an automatic response because automatic responses are well ingrained within us and can cause problem-atic behaviors. I am not particularly proud of it, but my automatic response was not super positive.

Screw them and screw this stupid project; I should just quit, I huffed to myself. Wow, this was a strong reaction! My immediate interpretation of the meaning of these emotions was that I should react, and *boy, did I*. I pulled all 150 lbs of Murphy closer, and for a moment, I sat still with the thought of quitting.

Would quitting further my overall goal at this moment? I wondered out loud. The goal was to tackle this project, to put into writing how to cope with mental health proactively in a way that brings more value and meaning to our lives—how to cope effectively with *all* the challenges we all face. Keeping that perspective in mind, reacting to rejection by quitting did not seem to fit. So, I took a step back and asked myself again, what is this telling me?

I sat in silence with myself until suddenly, it started to materialize for me. I did indeed want to react, but I did not want to react by quitting; I wanted to react by standing up for what I believed to be true, important, and meaningful, regardless of whether the regional TEDx organizers agreed or not. After I sat with these feelings and listened to them, I realized I wanted to react by continuing to tread this murky path forward.

Our automatic reaction is not always the whole story, which is why sitting with it and being curious about it pays off. Our feelings often have multiple layers, and we must listen intently to decode their meaning. Once I recognized that the feeling was calling on me to act, it was a quick jump to identifying the needed action as reinvesting in this project. I was motivated by this realization and found myself packing up my laptop on a dreary Wednesday and heading to the local coffee shop where, espresso and almond croissant in hand, I took the difficult first step of reengaging with this work. Of course, it didn't hurt that the walk to the coffee shop had helped me soothe the residual emotional discomfort and helped energize me for the work ahead—a happy reminder of the efficacy of one of my favorite coping skills.

So, there I was, consciously coping, able to shift myself away from old patterns to focus on coping in such a way that it progressed me towards my goals. My best life. *My peace of mind.* I could have shut it down, I could have quit at the first sign of discouragement, but the truth is I'd spent the last ten years doing that, and it hadn't gotten me anywhere meaningful. Instead, it had caused me more challenges.

I had learned an important coping lesson, one I wanted to capture for future reference, to remind me what I do when I fail. I pick up and I move forward, or I shut down. Although there is a distinct sting in failure, I know that the feeling of empowerment that comes from perseverance not only heals that sting but *brings me so much more overall.* This insight has increased my resilience to failure and the inherent value I see in failure. This was not an easy lesson to learn, and it is still one I struggle with, but over time and through practice, that struggle has become less cumbersome. I had learned from my previous failures how to cope most effectively with future failures.

Through this process of paying attention to and learning from yourself, the ongoing work of effective coping demonstrates its value. The more you practice this process, the more skilled you become at piecing together important patterns, themes, triggers, and narratives about yourself and your world, and suddenly those meaningless instances start to reveal meaningful patterns.

Although the rejection from TEDx still bothers me a bit, it did not consume me, nor did it shut me down. In fact, by paying attention to it, I re-engaged this project in a meaningful way. This experience helped me understand how you can consciously cope with a challenging moment. I now feel grateful for the rejection, as it gave me something far more important than the external validation I initially sought out. It allowed me to remember something fundamental. The validation I needed to cope with the vulnerability connected to a project like this book didn't need to come from some external source like the regional TEDx organizers. *The validation I sought was within me.*

I had coped effectively with the sting of rejection; so effectively that it has catapulted me to this moment. This moment when I am living my dream, as you are reading my book. Isn't it funny how present setbacks can turn into tomorrow's triumphs? Life is wonderfully uncertain like that.

I can cope with tough things just as well as you can cope with tough things. The difference is I've learned how to consciously pay attention to how I am coping, hone my skills to improve my overall coping efficacy, and most importantly, I have embraced the secret to your mental health.

There is no perfect mental health. Stop trying to make it a thing. The narrative that some human out there doesn't experience some degree of anxiety or depression, communication problems with their partners or families, trauma, loss, or grief, or doesn't need help from others emotionally is total baloney. *Let that junk go.*

Embracing this secret has transformed my mental health. It has softened my approach to my myself. It is not a flaw within me that needs to be removed; it is a complex, beautiful distillation of me that just craves to be understood, loved, and supported. This book is my gift to share what I have learned about coping and how conscious coping can decrease your distress and increase your contentment. I can think of no better gift to give to myself or anyone else than to support their journey towards conscious coping.

Straight out of the gate, here are 11 truths about coping

1. Everyone has the ability to cope and is actively coping all the time.

2. Coping is neither good nor bad; coping just is and thus can only be assessed by being more effective and less effective.

3. How you cope is uniquely personal; how you cope from time to time, moment to moment, is apt to change as well. If you aren't hurting yourself or anyone else, you have carte blanche to cope however you need to cope.

4. You are the *only* expert on you and how you cope. No one can do the hard work of learning how to cope for you, and if you are doing it right, you'd never want them to.

5. Coping is interdisciplinary and improvisational; it is an art form involving multiple skill sets to solve problems dynamically and critically.

6. Coping happens in both your brain and your body. Your brain is in your body, and your body is in your brain; part of coping with your mental health is taking care of your physical health as well.

7. We don't have to know "why" things happen to cope (although it is nice if we do); coping is about finding internal ways to cope with challenging things. Not assigning blame.

8. We cope with both "positive" and "negative" things; it's just that our brain tends to focus on the negative or complex coping challenges we face.

9. Curiosity is key to effective coping.

10. We are built to cope; many of our default coping procedures can be automated, but just because you can cope on autopilot doesn't mean it's the healthiest choice. Effective coping is active.

11. There is no "perfect" coping; we cope how we cope.

There were only supposed to be ten truths, but I guess it's appropriate that the one addressing my perfectionism put me over the top!

How You Cope Matters

I used to think of coping as if I were on a tightrope. You are either *on* or *off*. But coping is not so binary. Coping is active. Coping is more like a seesaw. It takes energy to balance actively. It takes energy to cope. Coping is about the act of balancing, *not* absolute balance.

It is about constant adaptability, and most importantly, it's about *your confidence in your ability to do so*. We cope with so many things in life. In general terms, we are tasked with coping whenever we have an emotional response. Which, regardless of who you are, adds up to a lot of coping. I'm sure this may seem quite overwhelming at first, but it's important to note that most things that you cope with will not require as much attention and time as I described in my experience of rejection above. In fact, effectively coping can be a quick, efficient process.

Conversely, when we do not manage our coping proactively, we can set ourselves up for a long and painful process. The goal is to untie the knot as soon as we notice it is tightened, not to wait until one knot transforms into a mega knot with no clear start or end. That being said, as long as you are intentional (and self-disciplined enough to handle it in a timely manner), it is perfectly acceptable to wait for a specific tool or outside help or just take a *beat*.

This model is focused on what is the most effective way to cope. That means that although best practice is to cope in the moment, coping tomorrow when you can call your best friend, or next week when you know the results of your lab work, or even avoiding it until you can get into a safe situation may be the most effective ways to cope. Ineffective ways to cope include avoiding it because you don't care, can't be bothered, or don't know what to do otherwise. *The key is your intention*; effective coping requires you to show up, be present in your life, and mindfully pay attention to how you are coping, not that you do it on a specific timeline.

As a psychotherapist, I have been privileged to work with many people who are in the process of learning how to cope more effectively. Most of them started from a place of paying little if any attention to how they were coping. If we aren't paying attention to how we are coping and its efficacy, we can't consciously learn how to cope more effectively. What a lost opportunity! But there is good news: all you have to do is pay attention to how you are coping to reclaim this opportunity. And the better news? You can start right now, this instant; you can show up for yourself and give yourself the best gift of all—your attention.

Coping is a constant; life continually gives us challenges, and we must continually cope with them. There are so many things in life with which we must cope—an infinite number of challenging opportunities that we encounter constantly. How we are coping with things is essential information. When we look at these responses as qualitative data points, we can approach them in a curious, non-judgmental way. Within them is knowledge you can choose to integrate or discard, but you must examine it first to know how to proceed. Otherwise, it is just noise.

Think about it like this: imagine everything you must cope with comes through as a piece of mail. When you are coping consciously, you open the mail, read it, analyze it, and decide what you need to do with it. Based on that decision, you either file the letter away (for future knowledge or reference), put it in a to-do pile (to act), or shred it if it was junk data. (Junk data happens when we cope with something fake. For example, if I am having a tough morning because I had dreamed my friend did something awful to me and I am coping with my anger towards her, I am dealing with junk data. I still need to cope with the anger, which is real and valid because I feel it. I also need to remind myself that she did not do the awful things I saw her do in my dreams. Junk data represents real things you must cope with, but due to unreliable, or in this case purely imaginative sources, there is nothing more to do about it other than just to feel the feeling.)

Let's say one day you just decide to stop getting the mail. You decide that this mail has no value, is not worth your time or energy, or for whatever reason, neglect it. Instead of being proactive, you just react; every time you get a piece, you crumple it up and throw it on the floor. Pretty soon, your floor is cluttered with mail; suddenly, this cluttered and uncertain state starts to cause you distress, primarily because it is a constant reminder of something you need to do for yourself *but are not doing.* You are surrounded by emotional clutter. It drains you to be living in this room filled with unopened mail, but you continue to ignore it. Slowly, you gain the energy to deal with some of it, but then there is one pile of unfinished business that you will not even acknowledge, let alone tackle. Finally, one day you find yourself screaming at the mailbox for continuing to deliver mail while you are drowning in your inability to deal with it. It is not the mailbox's fault; your energy is misguided, and the mailbox is the easiest scapegoat for the unease you have created by not dealing with the issues at hand.

When was the last time you went to your mailbox?

If, by chance, it has been a while, I have fantastic news: you can still catch up on all that mail! However, it will take time, energy, patience, intention, and work to do so. It will require more than if you dealt with this mail in the moment. By neglecting your coping mailbox, there is a decent chance you have developed some ineffective coping strategies. Coping happens regardless of whether we are paying attention or not. The problem with this is that without us giving it much thought, we can be making ineffective coping choices that can further negatively impact our mental health. Automatic coping tends to lead to you cleaning up an overwhelming mess of mail. That being said, *it's a mess you can clean up*, and once you do so, you get into a healthier routine and can attend to your coping mailbox in real-time.

You are always coping. The question is, are you paying attention to it? While coping is a constant, its efficacy is not. If you aren't paying attention to it, your efficacy suffers. When your coping is ineffective, your mental health is negatively impacted.

The Connection Between Coping and Your Mental Health

Coping refers to how we manage, care for, and deal with our mental health and everything connected to it. Our mental health is an essential part of our experience as humans. We cannot deny it, and to do so would make any type of effective coping impossible. Denying your mental health is unhealthy and unhelpful. Even if you don't qualify for a mental health diagnosis such as depression, anxiety, schizophrenia, you will still struggle with your mental health. *But there is nothing wrong with me,* you may be thinking. You are right! There is nothing wrong with you; instead, something is *right* with you. You live your life and feel your feelings, but if you don't know how to cope with those feelings, it can often feel like you are doing something wrong. That's because we often assume uncomfortable emotions are "wrong" or "bad" emotions. It's a path of least resistance for the brain to connect these things; you must learn to build comfort in dealing with discomfort to cope effectively.

Our brain *really* likes patterns, so it actively seeks to simplify anything into a pattern. To our brain, simple is good; everything should be as simplified as possible. When things are simple, it is easier to do the complex decision-making we are tasked with doing throughout our day-to-day. Also, our brain often erroneously thinks that keeping things simple is protecting us from threats. Because of the attempted simplicity of this process, many of us have learned that discomfort is bad news.

Discomfort isn't inherently bad, just as it isn't inherently good. We are tasked with helping our brain deal with our mental health compassionately and proactively in practical ways. To do so, we must guide it beyond our instinctual, default, automatic ways of coping, which in itself will cause discomfort. It is only when we lean into that discomfort that we can fully reap the power of our mental health. Our mental health is our key barometer for navigating the good stuff like balance, belonging, meaning, and joy.

Our brain is an amazing thing, but we cannot genuinely talk about coping if we don't first acknowledge our complex dual relationship with it. We are simultaneously the users and the researchers of it. There is much to be learned about our brain. At this moment in time, we know more about it than we have ever known before. That being said, it would be a mistake to think our brains are perfect or infallible. They are amazing, AND they can fall victim to learning errors. It takes critical thought to sort through how to cope most effectively. The thing is, though, critical thinking takes energy, and in our over-extended, chronically stressed and overwhelmed, even desperate times, most of us just say *phooey!* We don't have the energy to do that! Pay attention ourselves? Manage our mental health? Cope with life effectively? I can't even find the time to eat and sleep, let alone consciously care for myself!

It is, in some ways, a fair response. I mean, I get it. An infinite number of things need our energy, and our energy is finite; our needs are often at the end of our own list. But the thing is, to be thoroughly checked in and ready to deal with the path ahead, you must pay attention to your mental health and how you are coping. To give your best to those people and things in your life, you must care for the machine creating the energy. You must take care of yourself and your mental health.

That's where coping comes in. We can either cope in ways that are more healthy and helpful to our mental health or in ways that are, in the long-term, unhealthy or unhelpful to us. When you are angry, you can take a walk to cope, caring for your body, recharging your energy, and releasing your anger, or you can punch the wall and break your hand, resulting in a trip to the hospital, medical bills, rehab, and more challenges to your mental health. Which path do you think was more effective? Which one do you think your brain would be more apt to choose if you were triggered and angry?

It should be noted that neither of these reactions is right nor wrong; it's just that one is a more conscious reaction to coping. While the walk represents a short-term triumph, that does not mean the incident with the wall is worthless. It could be the setback that translates into you asking for help and starting the journey towards meaningful change. Conscious coping is as much about mindful, proactive, and critical decision-making when it comes to how you cope as it is about honoring the strength and resilience rooted in all our attempts to cope, no matter how effective or ineffective. *Our ability to cope is dazzling.*

Professionally I have found that the two most significant predictors of success when it comes to effective coping is someone is paying attention to their mental health and believing that they can cope. That's the baseline; conscious coping cannot happen without these things. More factors support conscious coping, which we will get into shortly, but for now, this is an important point I need you to sit with. The price of admission to the world of effective coping is paying attention to yourself, caring for your mental health, and believing in your ability to cope. *Can you stomach that cost?* I hope you can.

Effective vs. Ineffective Coping

We can cope with challenging things ineffectively if we aren't paying attention. We can run from them, avoid them, invalidate them, laugh at them, numb them, or just burn the whole thing down to annihilate them. Yet, inevitably, there you will be, standing amidst your own devastation. The challenge will not go away until you address it. No matter the matches and gasoline you throw onto it, it will not diminish without your intentional intervention.

That is coping ineffectively. Often this is the worst-case scenario. Sometimes, the automatic responses lead us down this path; sometimes, it happens because we don't know how or don't think we can cope. I'm here to tell you that you can cope with tough things, and building more tools and structures can support you in your ability to do so. *You can do this*, but you'll waste your energy if you don't believe you can.

That's what happened to me after my father's death; I was stuck, frozen in time and terror, unable to comprehend my ability to cope. Well, in truth, I was coping, my brain was protecting me, but this process was happening automatically. My subconscious took over, and I was numbed out. I was but a tourist in my own life, stopping to comment on things of interest but not interested in anything other than instant gratification. Food, booze, drugs, I didn't mind as long as it shielded me from the grief and trauma raging inside of me. It was horribly ineffective coping. My relief was momentary at best, and the costs of numbing were significant. *I lost time.* Yet as much as it kept me away from my grief, I knew instinctively that facing it was the only way to heal enough to continue my forward progression in life.

Grief and trauma can tell us that we don't deserve, won't have, or can't handle a life beyond these tough things, but those thoughts are wrong. Well-meaning saboteurs want to keep you shielded from the pain and, by default, rob you of the opportunity to triumph through your challenges. Grief and trauma are painful, *but there is always a path forward.* You may not see it yet if you are in it, but that does not mean it will not be there. There will come a time when you will be able to see the gift of your grief or trauma. You may detest the packaging, but it is a gift from the universe nonetheless.

Conscious coping is about honoring these things, making space for them, continually tending to them as needed, but ultimately not letting them derail our forward progress. The challenges you have faced are destinations along your journey, *not the journey itself.*

It is important to practice self-compassion when it comes to coping. We are adaptive and resilient beings, and we humans have found many unique ways to survive, but sometimes those survival skills cause us more harm or don't serve us in the long term. Coping, after all, is just learned skills and responses, and if something can be learned, it can be unlearned.

When we look at coping through the lens of efficacy, instead of "right" or "wrong," we can limit self-judgment and prompt conscious decision-making about how we are coping. Additionally, we leave conscious space for certain types of coping to be effective in one situation while less effective in others.

Some examples of effective coping include:

- Asking for help

- Talking about your feelings

- Leaning into your support system and encouraging them to lean into you as well

- Using coping skills to help you manage and recharge your energy levels

- Practicing both internal and external compassion

- Allowing yourself to have some fun!

Some examples of ineffective coping include:

- Yelling at the coffee shop barista on your way to a stressful meeting to cope with the anger and tension you feel towards your boss.

- Giving a lavish present to your friend with the hopes that she will avoid confronting you about the mean things you said to her when you were drunk. If she avoids it, you don't have to deal with the embarrassment and shame you feel.

- Asking others to tell you your work is "good enough" to sidestep giving yourself that validation because, at your core, you don't think you deserve it or are scared you do or are otherwise blocked from telling yourself how freaking awesome you are!

- Giving a public apology to someone as a means of putting a band-aid on your relationship, as it is what you think you should do or what others tell you should do. Frankly, you just want to move on because you are unable or unwilling (or both) to manage and cope with an actual conflict with this other party. In other words, you are sweeping it under the rug, but eventually, we move the rug, and we have to deal with what's underneath. Sooner or later, *your choice.*

- Not doing anything and just shutting down.
- Numbing by drinking (or drugging, sexting, shopping, exercising, obsessing, gambling, harming, or anything else that can trigger a neuro-chemical response) to escape from the intensity of it all.
- Finding yourself hyper-vigilant, always looking for the exits, the worst-case scenarios, the next fight, and chronically over-reacting or reacting aggressively.
- Not leaving your house so you don't have to deal with the panic you feel socially.

Remember that when we are coping ineffectively, we are still coping; it's just that we are coping in ways that are problematic at best and antithetical at worst to our personal growth and progress. When we talk about ineffective coping, we are talking about specific dynamics including (but not limited to) using the wrong tools or tools that may further exacerbate whatever we are coping with (i.e., punching the wall), external validation (erroneously looking for external validation from others, when what you really need is internal validation from yourself), unchecked ego defenses (actively working to avoid the discomfort through deflecting your friend by buying them a present instead of taking ownership for your behaviors and feelings your feelings), misplaced coping (not coping with the core issue, like being stressed out and angry at your boss), protective coping (coping how you or others think you should cope, disregarding your own experience), immature coping (not knowing how to cope or having a structure for coping), and trauma/grief response coping (in which the more primitive, safety-focused part of your brain is just trying to find safety and stability).

These are just some of the challenging dynamics that can twist and morph our coping methods if we aren't paying attention. Regardless of what you choose, how effective or ineffective, how you cope impacts your mental health.

How is Conscious Coping Different?

As I've already started to explain, there is a different, more empowering approach to coping than just leaving our brain to learn and react without a helpful framework in place. I call this framework EMBRACE, which stands for ENGAGE, MONITOR, BRIEF, REFLECT, ABSORB, CAPTURE, ENDURE. EMBRACE is a seven-step process to conscious coping. Conscious coping refers to a mindful, compassionate, growth based and proactive approach to coping. In other words, conscious coping is effective coping; I will use these terms interchangeably throughout. In its essence, EMBRACE itself is ultimately an act of mindful meaning-making. By intentionally shining a light on how you cope with all the challenges, chaos, and uncertainty the universe provides, you have an opportunity to learn from them. And when you do, you can discover ways to make your coping even more effective tomorrow or the next time you encounter a similar challenge. If we take the time to consciously care for our mental health today, not only can we reduce our distress now, but we can also learn ways to reduce our distress in the future.

EMBRACE is grounded in a growth-based mindset that values the innate opportunities present within the challenges we face. It normalizes the ongoing work required to develop these skills and celebrates the strengths and resilience within all of us. When one is consciously coping, one chooses to engage in mindful, ongoing experiential learning about how they, as unique individuals, cope most effectively with all the challenges, chaos, and uncertainty surrounding them. The goal is to increase one's confidence in their ability to cope, as actively believing one can cope with tough things is a mental health prophylactic[3].

Or, in more poetic terms:

Conscious coping
is the balance you will find,
when you pay attention to your mind,
and treat yourself kind.

Conscious coping also makes space for coping with tough things. I'm not here to BS you or paint a toxically positive picture here. No sir. It would be against my existentialist belief system to not acknowledge the true human experience. It is an uncomfortable truth that awful things can happen, but infinite wells of opportunity can spring from those awful things. I can't gloss over the fact that grief and trauma are ever-present in our world. I can't ignore that there are seemingly insurmountable things that our world expects

---

3   Roman Cieslak, Charles C Benight, and Victoria Caden Lehman, "Coping Self-Efficacy Mediates the Effects of Negative Cognitions on Posttraumatic Distress," *Behaviour Research and Therapy* 46, no. 7 (July 2008): 788–98, https://doi.org/10.1016/j.brat.2008.03.007.

us to cope with. I can't lie and say I've never thought nope, I can't cope with this, because I have. But I can say whether you think you can cope or think you can't makes all the difference. And the truth is we can cope with tough things. Look around: the evidence of this is within us all.

There are moments in life when you cannot cope *at the moment* because something happened that overwhelmed you. Please know two things. First, this is part of our brain's evolved ability to disassociate when there is acute pain, but, and this is very important, we aren't wired to do this for the long haul. Secondly, just because you weren't able to cope then doesn't mean you can't cope now or in the future. Be patient with yourself; when your sense of safety and security is rattled even slightly, it takes time to re-calibrate.

As awful as grief and trauma are, an amazing gift comes with them, but you must cope effectively to grasp it. That gift is meaning-making. Meaning-making is the process of making sense of challenging things that have happened in a way that brings value and insight into how you see yourself and your world. Conscious coping makes space for life's many challenges and honors the roles of grief and trauma within our lives.

After years of being faced with tough things and communing with others about tough things, I have come to accept those tough things happen, and they aren't going to stop. I have come to accept the absurd. That within these tough things lie great value. We triumph when we can unearth that value. I know it sounds bonkers, but it is true. It is true for me because I can earnestly say to you my father's suicide brought value to my life. I don't like it, I wouldn't have chosen it, I wouldn't call it a "good thing," but I've accepted that the way I have shown up and made meaning from this catastrophic loss has been a significant driver of my personal growth and success. My father's suicide was the most devastating thing I have ever faced, AND it was the launching point for many of my triumphs. A significant source of healing and personal empowerment can be traced directly back to my most considerable trauma. My father's suicide was catastrophic, AND I am proud of how I continue to cope with it. The great opportunity for me has been to commit to being part of the conversation about mental health as a means to honor him and his life. It's uncomfortable, but these opposing things are both true. My brain helps me find that deep, meaningful insight, but my brain also struggles to cope with it. That's why it's so important to intentionally support it.

Our mental health is a fire raging within us. Ideally, it is but a pilot light, but you must pay attention to it to ensure it doesn't become a conflagration. Conscious coping is about paying attention to that fire, stoking it, tempering it, honoring it, and as needed, wielding it effectively. Due to the challenge, chaos, and uncertainty that the universe provides, tending to the fire is dynamic. In other words, due the constant of change we face, how we cope needs to be more improvisational than absolute.

When we improvise, we address a problem proactively with the tools immediately at hand. Improvisation is an important skill, and the more we practice it, the more tolerant we are to uncertainty. When I joined the improv team in college, my father haughtily suggested that I move on to a different, more meaningful hobby after a year. He would say, *how much more could you learn from improv after one year?* I like to think of this memory because if he were here now, I would tell him he was wrong. My four years of improv in college were the playground for me to develop my most valuable skill set. Improvisation. So much of what we do in life is improvised, and improvising is a big part of my confidence in my ability to cope. Also, to be honest, as a psychotherapist, I never know what is going to "walk through my door" on any given day. Thus, improvisation has been essential to my career.

You do not have to join an improv troupe to practice improv, and you do not have to be funny doing it, but you do have to connect with your natural ability to improvise because it is an essential part of tending to the fire of your mental health. We want to tend that fire effectively for as long as we can so that when it is time for it to be extinguished, we have developed our abilities to pass that learning on to others. It is the only thing we owe to each other, to those before and after us. To continue learning how to cope with life so that the human race continues to triumph, that is the only way for us all to progress.

On a personal note, I like to think that at the end of my journey, when my own pilot light is extinguished (or transformed? or if the universe is taking requests carried into the next nebula by a giant space turtle as we rock out to REO Speedwagon?), I will be willing and able to express my gratitude for my imperfect, challenging mental health. It is a gift to experience our mental health, learn about it, and cultivate ways to cope with it; doing so drives us towards our purpose and meaning and makes the ride a lot more fun.

You've worked hard to get to this point, where you are reading a book on how you can take better care of your mental health. I hope you take this opportunity to cope more effectively, in whatever format that takes. I hope you join me on this journey to conscious coping.

CHAPTER 2

Foundations of
Conscious Coping

To grow your beautiful coping garden, we must first cultivate the right soil. The soil in this context is made up of many different things. Still, it must include compassion, a growth-focused mindset, validation, inner experience, resilience to discomfort, vulnerability, radical acceptance of (uncomfortable) truths, and realistic expectations. Everyone's soil is unique, and it is important to understand which of these things you have in abundance and which of these you must work to cultivate more of.

Before we assess your soil, you need to ask yourself something. *Have you committed to taking care of this garden?* It is one thing to till the earth, test the soil, and plant the plants those first few days, but what happens when the scorching July sun glares down, and your garden beckons for you to tend to it, care for it, protect it in its time of need? Are you prepared to commit to the ongoing maintenance to reap not only the bountiful harvest but also the mindful journey of doing so?

No judgment here: I'm asking as someone who has planted a glorious garden a time or two, only to neglect it when the going got tough. That was ineffective coping. Now I try and prioritize the seemingly insignificant day-to-day, moment-to-moment tasks required to keep my coping garden flourishing. In more practical terms, we are talking about mental health hygiene. Before we tend to the soil, let's take a moment to reflect on what it means to commit to our mental health hygiene.

Committing To Your Mental Health Hygiene

You have control over your behaviors. It is one of the few things you have total control over. You cannot control your feelings, you cannot control others, you can control your thoughts only a little bit, so what remains is your behavior. Your behavior, in this case, is how you care for yourself. Coping is an area where you have complete control. By growing your ability to cope and increasing your confidence in coping in the future, you have engaged in preventative mental health care.

Coping is to mental health, as brushing your teeth is to oral health. Your mental health hygiene matters. The most amazing thing about us humans is positive choices tend to have an amplifying impact on us, wherein one positive health choice tends to beget more. Of course, the opposite is also true, which is why we must be careful of the tools we use. Avoidance of one thing can easily lead to avoidance of *all things*.

When you acknowledge the control you have over your behaviors and how they can impact your ability to care for yourself and your mental health, you step into a place of empowerment. When we are empowered to take care of ourselves, the barriers decrease. Your behaviors are how you demonstrate your commitment to caring for your mental health.

For a long time, I would dread going to the dentist. The dentist, to me, was an overwhelming space full of loud noises, uncomfortable sensations, bright lights, and an inevitable shame spiral. All these things are objectively true about the dentist; everything except for the shame spiral, which was something entirely of my own making. I have always struggled to engage in good oral hygiene, and though I don't know why, it's been a consistent challenge for me. I even feel shame right now as I type this out. As a dentist appointment loomed on my calendar, I would try and "make up" for all the missed daily hygiene tasks I had neglected, with the hope that I could fool the dentists and the hygienists and hide the fact that I had not been taking care of my oral health on a day-to-day basis. *Fun fact*, dentists and dental hygienists know that you are full of fibs when you tell them you floss every day. The proof is, of course, in the pudding, or in this case, *in the tartar.*

At a certain point, as an adult responsible for the costs and pain that resulted from not taking care of myself daily, I decided that I needed to change my behavior and start tackling the challenge of taking care of my oral health. Since I have done so, I have experienced a spectacular shift when I go to the dentist; although the loud noises, uncomfortable sensations, and bright lights are all still present, I do not have to deal with the shame spiral because every day I have done what I needed outside of the dentist's office to take care of myself.

Mental health is the same. You must work at it every day; in fact, you must work at it multiple times throughout the day. The thing is, though, that when you manage it proactively, you do not have to be consumed by it. If you have ever experienced depression or anxiety, or another type of mental health crisis, you know how consuming it can be. Of course, it is work that you must engage in every day, but the small, incremental daily work is much easier to manage than the overwhelming work that presents after a crisis. Remember, though, no matter the crisis, there is a way through. You *can* cope with tough things.

I want to say when you come to an appointment with your mental health professional, and you tell us that you "have been taking care of yourself," and in truth, you haven't been, we can usually see through your fibs, as well. No judgment: we all struggle in this area. Do not waste your time or energy; you do not need to lie to us about it.

Compassion

Now that we have established your commitment to tend to your coping garden, we can move on to assessing your soil. A healthy dose of compassion, particularly self-compassion, can be the hardest fundamental to come by, but its power is astounding. When I struggle to be compassionate with myself, here is a trick I use. Our mind is a tool of such great power that it is mostly a mystery. Think about this: the brain is the most complex thing in the known universe, and we are simultaneously the users of it and are also its researchers. This is a helpful thought for me when I struggle or judge myself for my imperfections. It grounds me in humility and realistic expectations for myself and keeps me from spinning into spirals of overwhelm, shame, and self-annihilation.

Compassion is the gentle reminder that we are all in this great unknown together. If we can do anything to reduce the suffering for ourselves or others, it is *usually* worth doing. Please note this does not mean that we would do anything to reduce the suffering of ourselves or others. By being mindful of how our thoughts and actions contribute to the suffering of ourselves and others, our default should be to err on the side of reducing suffering when possible. In other words, I will not go rob a bank to decrease your financial suffering, but I will not judge you for having anxiety about your financial struggle. If I can support you through my words or actions, like helping you find a financial counselor or listening to you when you need to vent, I will do so if it does not violate my conscience or your agency.

Compassion for others is a vital part of conscious coping. If we can all agree that mental health is challenging and that we all struggle with it, we can sidestep all the needless external and internal judgment we've bludgeoned ourselves with. Judging ourselves for our imperfect nature, as well as judging others for their mental health challenges, are both wastes of energy. We have allowed this judgment to permeate our culture. Generations of people have been taught to ignore, invalidate, and demean themselves. This is the grandest example of ineffective coping I can point to.

The opposite of compassion is heartlessness. When we are heartless, we do not value our shared humanity, we do not look to lighten the load of ourselves or others, and in extreme cases, we will engage in cruelty through our willing contribution to the suffering of others. When you are compassionate, you are not looking for someone to blame; you accept that things are outside all our control, and you work to lighten a load of you and everyone around you when it is appropriate to do so. When you exhibit heartlessness, you carry cruelty with you and dole it out to yourself and anyone around you. I have always found, personally and professionally, that when you carry around heartlessness, you are also carrying around hurt. I am not sure what type of hurt you may or may not be caring with you, but you have permission to put it down. Unresolved hurt begets heartlessness, and heartlessness begets *more* heartlessness.

Usually, compassion towards others is easier for most of us than compassion towards ourselves. We haven't been taught that it is proper to have compassion towards ourselves. Further, because we live day in day out with our imperfect mental health, we know it all: the good, the bad, and the ugly. As a result, we are quicker to paint a negative picture of who we are. Self-compassion is a key tool, especially when it comes to energy management. Judging yourself takes a lot of energy. Instead of using your energy to beat yourself up, use that energy to lift yourself up by being compassionate with yourself. Compassion for yourself and compassion for others are inextricably tied no matter their proximity to you. If we practice compassion towards ourselves, it is easier to practice it towards others and vice versa.

Compassion does not mean that we excuse or accept behaviors and actions that are inappropriate or harmful; instead, it seeks to understand the humanity of the circumstances that surround such things. Sometimes the most compassionate thing we can do for someone is to hold them accountable for their actions in a way that clearly and transparently communicates our reasons for doing so. People need to grow and learn in life, and accountability is an important part of the picture.

When I was in graduate school, one of my internships sites was the local mental health court. During my time there, I encountered many individuals who had done awful, sometimes horrific things to their family, friends, and themselves. It took a lot of external and internal exploration on my part to reconcile the person who had done these awful things with the person sitting before me trying to get better and change. My job was not to make their stint in mental health court *easier* for them. I couldn't do that regardless, but if I had been able to, that would have been the opposite of me being compassionate to them. There were important lessons, skills, and experiences for them to absorb. Compassion instead looked like providing them with acceptance and allowing them to talk about and explore the pain they had caused themselves and others without judgment. Compassion was validating how challenging the whole situation was, reminding them that they were not alone and that there was hope beyond the challenge of right now. Compassion was holding them accountable for the actions that had led them to the court and talking about the tough stuff to make the most out of their opportunity to grow within this challenge. Compassion was treating them kindly even when they weren't kind to me.

Kindness is the behavioral act of compassion—kindness matters, especially when it is not reciprocated. People do lots of in-congruent things in life, and one of the greatest examples of this is how *hurt people* tend to *hurt other people*. The flawed logic is that if I feel this way, others should feel that way, or I can reclaim my power by hurting others. When people treat you in an unkind or disrespectful manner, there is a particularly good chance that the root of their behaviors has more to do with them than it does with you. Keep in mind you can be kind while still having boundaries and being mindful of your personal safety and security.

Compassion is key to conscious coping because it grounds you in your imperfect nature and the very real challenges we all face when dealing with our mental health amid chaos and uncertainty. Grounding our coping in compassions provides us with an accessible path towards developing and maintaining a growth-focused mindset.

Maintain A Growth Focused Mindset

A growth-focused mindset happens when we lean into our challenges and focus not on our mistakes but on what we can learn from them. When we have a growth-focused mindset, we tend to look past the challenges themselves as the metrics of our success and instead look to how we coped, what we learned, what we gained. With a growth-focused mindset, we also take time to compassionately acknowledge what we have lost when we have coped ineffectively.

With a growth-focused mindset, we look out for and take opportunities to grow through life and all the challenges we face. This mindset helps to prevent us from engaging in ineffective coping patterns including, but not limited to, avoiding, blaming, and invalidating. Keep in mind that you cannot tamp your feelings down; the more you push them down, the more they morph and metastasize within you in complex and insidious ways. The end result is someone who has become a husk of themselves, smothered by the simmering presence of any number of emotions, with anger, sadness, regret, terror, and shame being the heavy hitters. Take a moment and think of who you have encountered who has demonstrated this concept to you. Perhaps it was someone you know well or someone you met in passing. Perhaps all or part of yourself has been consumed like this, either in the past or present.

Once you have the image of that person in your head, take a moment and express compassion towards them. Of course, you must find out how you express compassion towards others. I take a moment to commune with them, to hold space within myself and consciously reflect on them, their humanness and the complex beauty within them, and then say (to myself or, if appropriate and not totally creepy, to them), how much I appreciate them showing up to the game. No matter how great or how poorly they or anyone else thinks it's going. When we have a growth-focused mindset, the only metric that matters is that we keep at it; this is why it is so important to our soil.

If you are struggling to develop more of a growth-focused mindset within yourself, think about someone in your life who always encouraged you to take chances and learn. Who told you it was okay to make mistakes as long as you learned from them? Who made you feel safe enough to fail? Summon them to your mind and invite them along with you. Ask yourself, how would they encourage you? What would they say? What would they do? How would you feel if they were here now cheering you on, saying you can do this, you can cope effectively with tough things? Dive deep into what you see. We need their voice and presence with us as we journey ahead into conscious coping.

Validation

As humans, we have a habit of overvaluing external validation and undervaluing internal validation. It's a funny dynamic because these priorities are skewed. External validation is like fools' gold: sparkly, distracting, and in the grand scheme of things, of little value. On the other hand, internal validation is precious and of great value; it is *the real gold*. In general terms, "validation" in this context means that we are cosigning on the realness and legitimacy of your experience. Or at least that is what it *should* be, but since we are social and competitive beings, what this looks like is a culture that attempts to use external cues to demonstrate worth and validity. I mean, take one look at your shiny Instagram feed. You get it: external validation is about having other people validate your choices, thoughts, beliefs, and values in life. Whether it's your Outfit-Of-The-Day, your cleaning hack, your juicy booty, your shiny new car, or even your well-behaved family, all of them are external cues that we show to gain validation from others. It is instinctual to want external validation, but let's not get it twisted; external validation is not the type of validation you need to consciously cope.

It is internal validation that is key here.

When you rely on other people to decide your worth and value, you can't consciously cope. Any idea why? Because you won't have time; you'll be running yourself ragged maintaining your shiny facade, and you'll have no energy to deal with the mess inside. You can still seek and enjoy external validation, just don't rely on it. Your value is the most important thing you hold within you; don't pass it off to anyone else. You are the only one who can care for it the way it needs to be cared for.

If you need to cultivate more self-validation, start by checking in with yourself at least three times a day. Ask yourself, *how am I feeling*? Make sure you answer with a feeling word and name as many feelings as you can identify. After you have named what you are feeling, tell yourself that what you are feeling is valid. Full stop. No other commentary necessary, no qualifications, judgments, and most of all, no invalidation. I suggest you start with this strategy because most of us constantly invalidate our emotional experiences. We say things like, *I shouldn't feel that way*, or *It doesn't matter how I feel*, or *I must be crazy for feeling this way*, or my favorite, *I don't give a flip about my feelings*. This is where invalidation starts, and it spreads insidiously from there.

If you find yourself invalidating your feelings, then you know you've got an invalidation pattern. That's okay; most of us do. Telling yourself that what you experience is valid and stopping there is a powerful way to lean into validating yourself. You'll come to understand that validating yourself is far more beneficial than seeking validation from anyone else. It will feel uncomfortable at first, but lean in. Dealing with the discomfort of tending to your relationship with yourself is great practice for building your overall resilience to discomfort.

So how are you feeling right now?

Is that feeling *valid*?

Say it with me: "I am feeling {insert feeling word here} and that is totally real and valid."

Then give yourself a big hug or whatever you like to provide yourself with physical affection and sit with the feeling for as long as you need to sit with it. You are the only one who knows how long that needs to be. Trust yourself; your experience is valid, whatever it is.

Inner Experience

Internal validation is communicated to us through our inner experience. Before I go any further here, let's discuss self-talk and the context in which I refer to it throughout this book. Self-talk is a type of inner experience. Many people talk to themselves internally, which has also been referred to as "internal monologue," but not everyone does. Well, at least, it is my understanding that not everyone thinks the way I think. I'm not talking about opinions here; I'm talking about the actual process of how you think.

I struggle to wrap my head around this one. In fact, it took me 30 minutes of searching online to find the language to explore this concept with you. The magic question that got the internet to connect me to the work of psychologist Russel Hurlburt was, *what is the opposite of internal monologue?* Hurlburt has identified 5 types of inner experiences, of which inner speaking is only one. In addition to inner speaking, there is inner seeing (where images are the primary experience), inner feeling, sensory awareness, and unsymbolized thinking which is "a trickier concept to get your head around, but essentially a thought that doesn't manifest as words or images, but is undoubtedly present in your mind.[4]"

Ahoy! What an iceberg of an uncomfortable truth we have encountered. It's not just the content of our experiences that differ, but the mechanics that produce the aforenoted content as well. We live 100% of our time with ourselves; it is hard to imagine what it would be like to live without ourselves, let alone what it would be like to live in the complex ecosystem of someone else's mind. *It is unimaginable.* It has never been done and barring any major scientific breakthroughs, it does not appear that it will be done. For better or worse, we only know our own experience; *that's why we are the experts on ourselves.*

I'm most aware of how my brain works differently than others when it comes to driving. I think about the best route ahead of time; I brainstorm additional tasks and experiences I can have along the way. I like a well-thought-out, efficient ride. Not everyone does this. My husband gets in the car *to cruise.* He will take the scenic route every time. We achieved the same outcome, arriving at our destination safely, but the routes we travel to get there are vastly different (literally).

At first, I found this maddening, but over time I realized it was only maddening because I expected him to do it my way. When I stopped expecting him to do it my way and started to expect the realistic outcome that he would do it his way, it irked me a bit, but it stopped making me want to blow my top! It took a good amount of conscious coping to identify that the pattern of us having conflict

4   Kelly Oakes, "What the Voice inside Your Head Says about You," BBC Future, August 19, 2019, https://www.bbc.com/future/article/20190819-what-your-inner-voice-says-about-you.

in the car when he was driving was due to me having an unrealistic expectation for him *to think exactly how I think.* As I began to understand what had been happening, I was able to muddle together an important lesson for me to capture. It's okay for us, *all of us*, to have our unique processes for managing and caring for our minds, bodies, and spirits. That is perfectly acceptable. The most important thing here is that we validate everyone's unique process. For the purpose of this book, I am going to talk about self-talk, primarily because it is part of my inner experience. For the purpose of your journey, it does not matter what your inner experience looks like; all you need to do to consciously cope is familiarize yourself with it.

Build Your Resilience to Discomfort

Here's the deal: there is a lot of advertising money spent marketing to your desire to reduce your feelings of discomfort. *Trust me*; my first career was in market research. A lot of thought goes into messaging intended to get you to cope with your feelings of discomfort by opening your pocketbook. *No shade!* I get it; I also own a Snuggie because I'd like to reduce the inherent discomfort of having to shed my blanket to use my arms.

It's not *bad* to have solutions to life's discomforts. Certainly, finding innovative solutions and interventions for disease and disability show the other side of this coin. Amazing good can come from the human desire to reduce discomfort, AND it can be amazingly destructive. After all, part of what fueled the opioid epidemic was the desire to eliminate human pain. For many individuals and their families, the benefit of short-term pain relief resulted in the long-term cost of addiction. Don't get me wrong, sometimes, painkillers are the best solution, but those circumstances are narrow. Life is full of discomfort, after all. If we always seek to numb our discomfort, there is no other option than to be numb to our lives. This is an extremely costly pattern. Over time, over-numbing creates a feedback loop wherein we reduce our opportunities to practice resilience to discomfort.

If we are confident in our ability to feel uncomfortable, we can better withstand the inherent discomfort of certain emotional experiences. Take love, for instance—arguably the emotion that we hold in the highest regard. But if you have ever known love before, and I hope you have in any form, romantic, familial, fraternal, or with a pet, you know the flip side of love. The flip side is the terrifying reality that what you love so much is just part of our fragile world full of challenges, chaos, and uncertainty, and since these wonderful things had a beginning, alas, they too will have an end. I don't know about you, but this causes me significant discomfort. Yet I know I must learn to tolerate this horrifying reality to access all the other good stuff about love. I don't need to celebrate it, feed it, or do anything to address it further, but I do have to acknowledge it. To not do so would be to push the feeling down, keeping me stuck and unable to cope effectively. We must lean into discomfort and build our resilience to it. There is triumph in our ability to harness our discomfort into something which moves us forwards.

Vulnerability

In this case, the discomfort of the searing vulnerability we experience when we love someone or something in our lives dearly is a sign *that something is right*. If you have had this type of love in your life, you have been successful. Your automatic instinct, which told you to avoid the inherent discomfort of vulnerability, wanted you to shun love to protect yourself. But through effective coping, you were able to override that instinct and allow yourself to lean into love and allow the discomfort to be just part of the cost of admission. Accept the presence of the discomfort as a sign you are doing it right. Don't let it overwhelm or taint the rest of your experience. After all, everything is dual in nature; you can't have the sweet without the sour.

Vulnerability is a vital foundation of authentic relationships, and authentic relationships with others supports our ability to consciously cope. By being vulnerable, you can be your authentic self with others. You give yourself permission to take off your mask and ditch the socially informed facade we all carry around most of the time. This courageous act allows you to be open to growing and evolving within your relationship. If you can be authentic with others, you can be authentic with yourself.

We know instinctively when we are in authentic relationships. A special magic happens when we feel we can take our masks off and be our whole selves with someone. Sometimes we meet someone, and right away, we feel like we can be vulnerable and authentic with them; other times, it is a slow burn to get there, but when you find it, it is something to nurture.

If you do not have authentic relationships with others or have had difficulty developing them, rest assured that you can practice the skills of vulnerability and authenticity with yourself. Your relationship with yourself is your foundational relationship. The more you practice dealing with the discomfort of vulnerability and authenticity with yourself (yes, it still presents even when you are just dealing with yourself), the more you will be able to engage this skill with others.

When we are authentic in our relationships, we risk getting hurt. There are many of us who, after being hurt, have decided consciously (or unconsciously) that we will no longer be vulnerable or authentic in our relationships as a means of self-protection. Although this is a very human response, it is misguided. A decision like this means you will never grow within a relationship, which is a huge, missed opportunity for your mental health. When you cannot be vulnerable, you shut off your opportunity to communicate about what you are experiencing mentally or emotionally, limiting your ability to ask for help when you may need it.

These are reasons you need vulnerability in your external life, but you must be vulnerable with yourself first. You must be able to sit down (literally) and be alone with yourself and face whatever is there. You have to communicate with yourself in your unique way and lay yourself bare. You must have an authentic relationship with yourself to consciously cope, and that is only possible if you can be vulnerable with yourself.

Often when people are unable to be vulnerable with themselves, they overschedule themselves. They do whatever they need to do to keep busy, often to their detriment. I'm talking about scheduling Zoom meetings on vacation or obsessively volunteering even when you don't have any more time to give. If you find yourself in a pattern like that, it may be time for a soft or hard reset, something we will explore further in part two.

Practice Radical Acceptance of (Uncomfortable) Truths

In our lives, there are times when we have to hold space for things that make us uncomfortable. Sometimes these are things that we cannot change; sometimes, these things are contradictory or confusing; often, these things are existential in nature. I say hold space because parts of our brains struggle to process complex concepts, the likes of which we are destined to entertain. It takes energy to hold these truths and accept them to dive deeper into what we can change. By accepting these things as above our pay grade, we can prevent ourselves from wasting our energy trying to change them. This is also how we honor them. For whatever reason, we don't know the answers to all our questions, but the uncomfortable truth is that life would look entirely different if we did.

One way we will try to cope with the inherent challenge, chaos, and uncertainty in life is by trying to control every little detail. *I get it*, I've been there, but we all know it's a losing game. It's a great way to waste your energy and get very little return on your investment. Do you know why this never works? Because you can stay up all night and imagine all the different potential things that can happen tomorrow, and guess what? It won't look like you think it will look *because it never does*. It's true that you probably can, for the most part, correctly predict how some events will play out tomorrow, but down to every last detail? Always? *No way*. That is entirely unrealistic. Instead of trying to control everything or having a plan for whatever you think may go down, wouldn't it be better to focus on getting rest and recharging so you can better respond when that next need to cope pops up?

Also, it's worth noting that if you spend all of your time trying to control things, you miss out on the organic, memorable moments of life. We only get glimpses of the good stuff, like balance, belonging, meaning, and joy, but you have to be present to experience them. Trying to control the future prevents you from doing so. Trying to control things is an ineffective way to cope and a waste of energy. Part of conscious coping is being honest about the system we are all working within. A life full of challenge, chaos, and uncertainty, a life full of things outside your control.

Our brains like a binary: yes or no, in or out, up or down. Our brains like this because the simpler things are, the easier they are to predict, and our brain's foundational duty is to regulate our bodies and protect us from threats. We can't help this; it is what we are built to do. But to consciously cope, you must challenge that binary mode of thinking.

Our brain struggles when it encounters dialectics. Something is dialectical when two seemingly opposing things are both true. The purest example of this is I am happy, AND I am sad. It's confusing; it seems like it shouldn't happen, but yet it does. Even though my brain doesn't like it, that doesn't make it less accurate. Dialectical challenges present frequently, so frequently that I will denote them throughout the book with a capital "AND." We've already stumbled upon a few in earlier pages; they are uncomfortable, yes, but they can be tolerable. We just must learn to accept them.

As I mentioned earlier, my father taught me that what matters most in life is that you show up and try. It was a pillar to who he was as a parent. But yet my father completed suicide. He made a choice one day to no longer show up and try. It is antithetical to who I knew him to be, but it is true, nonetheless. And so herein, I arrive at an acutely uncomfortable set of opposing truths. I learned the importance of showing up in life from my father, AND my father chose not to show up to life one day, and he and everyone around him suffered a catastrophic loss.

My father was my greatest teacher of this value AND the greatest violator of it.

I hate this, but I must honor it. I spent years trying to run from it, numb it away, but yet it remains. I choose to honor it because when I let one opposing truth duke it other with another opposing truth in the abstract reaches of my mind, I get stuck. An internal stalemate, resulting in a full shutdown. I imagine if you saw it from the outside, you would see a distant person, huddled under the safety of her duvet, with an increasing mess encapsulating her until she couldn't even be seen among the chaos and the clutter. Hiding, trying to blunt the oppressive heaviness that results from avoiding coping with challenges. *An ineffective approach*, but I do have compassion for myself and my desire to find safety in those moments. I understand my desire to reject and avoid the heaviness of some of these truths, especially the existential ones.

It is important to mention here that the existentialists abhor suicide, especially Camus, who viewed it as a rejection of freedom. Frankl posited that suicide was an escape from solving the problem, an escape that unfortunately leaves the problem unsolved. Forever and in perpetuity, not just for the person who completes suicide, but for everyone connected directly and indirectly. I speak from intimate experience.

I must say that although I do also very strongly dislike suicide, I have a more nuanced view of it when it comes to end of life and palliative care. A few years back, I challenged myself to watch a documentary called *How to Die in Oregon* about a handful of terminally ill people in Oregon who would be taking their lives legally via new euthanasia laws. When I sat down to watch that documentary, I was angry. *Steaming angry.* It had shown up on my HBO feed for weeks, and I had cursed its presence, hating that a positive documentary about suicide would even exist. But I had felt pulled towards it like it was something I needed to watch. I was correct; it was. It made me realize that once again, everything is dual in nature. The role of suicide, in this context, was to help terminally ill people end things on their terms in the most meaningful way possible. I want to express my gratitude to the families and all parties involved in that documentary, their vulnerability, and their willingness to journey through one of life's hardest truths. All that begins shall end. Every single person who worked on that documentary gave me a gift. They helped me see something I could not see before: the dual nature of suicide. I could not and cannot argue against compassionate doctor-assisted euthanasia; I just believe that it is a tool with a very limited scope.

Regardless of whether you make that choice intentionally due to a terminal illness, eventually, one day, you will not be able to physically cope with whatever challenge you face, and you will die. I know; *I hate it too!* That being said, I do not intend to make you lose hope; this is the exact reason why we are here. In the time that we do have, the time blessed with the plentiful challenge, and by extension, opportunity, we are tasked with a choice. A choice to survive and react without thought or intention, destined to survive but not thrive. Or the alternative, through hard work, determination, intention, and compassion, a choice to triumph through our challenges by coping effectively. There is always hope, AND there is always a challenge ahead.

Here is the good news: we are all born with the ability to cope, and we are all born with the ability to cope effectively. Coping is uniquely personal. At its core conscious coping is about doing what feels supportive, helpful, and soothing to you. You don't need to cope for anyone else, so you have the freedom to *100% do you.* The flip side of this is that determining what works best for you is challenging work, but when you are doing it right, it's the type of work you want to be doing.

There is another uncomfortable truth we must discuss; many will try to convince you that they have the answers to what you need, but no one else can correctly answer these questions for you other than yourself. By all means, pick your teachers and call upon their teachings throughout your journey, but be mindful that absolute dedication to someone else's views invalidates your own experience, and your experience is always valid. *In other words, beware of one-size-fits-all options.*

It's not just the ease of taking on someone else's views that is tempting; it is also the very real shortcut it presents. We are addicted to the quick fix, the instant gratification, the perfect solution. Many people and institutions will try to tell you that they know more about you and your journey than you do. It is a scam; they do not.

All that being said, these people and institutions may bring immense value to your journey. You are free to use whatever teachers or tools you see fit, as long as you do so with intention. Organized religion is a good example of this: faith and religion bring significant meaning to many people's journeys. You can borrow from religion or even use it as a means to ground your ability to cope. You can be all in, all out, or any way in between, as long as you do the conscious work of connecting with those things for yourself. The moment you start parroting other people's beliefs, you've stopped consciously coping.

Because coping is so deeply personal, please keep in mind how I cope may not be effective for you, and vice versa. Further, how you cope in one moment or situation in your life is apt to be different in another moment. Coping is dynamic and responsive to your environment, history, genetics, family, pathology, trauma, and a million other data points. Remember there is no "right" or "wrong," only more effective and less effective. Please be compassionate with yourself and others regarding how you or they may have coped in the past. There is no need to judge yourself; let's harness that energy instead to brainstorm different ways to cope with similar things in the future. *That is how we consciously cope.*

So instead of absolute solutions, focus on helping yourself create your own framework for coping: one that is flexible enough to adapt to the constant challenge, chaos, and uncertainty but rigid enough to withstand them. This is a tremendous task, and as such, it is imperative that you develop, design, and implement this framework. You are, after all, the expert on you; another uncomfortable truth.

Strive For Realistic Expectations

Keep in mind that developing your ability to cope is an ongoing process. Given the constant of change, your need to cope never ends; therefore, your potential for growth is endless. Just because our potential for growth is endless does not mean that we have endless potential to enact change in our lives in any way we please. *No, ma'am.* That would be unrealistic. We have many frameworks that we have to work within. Existentially, physically, culturally, professionally, bureaucracies, systemic, family, and even in our peer groups, there are limited ways we can enact meaningful change in our lives in other to cope more effectively. You must have realistic expectations for yourself. You can only change some things, and even then, change takes time.

We need to be mindful that we do not control the timeline of our emotions. We can do certain things to encourage and discourage them to move along, but they are ultimately transient in nature. When they depart is outside our control. A week after my father's funeral, I sat in my then therapist's office and asked her, "I have a week between semesters. Can you give me a checklist to get through this grief in the next week? I'm really dedicated to getting it done quickly."

I can still see the perplexed look on her face as she quietly but assertively said, "No. It doesn't work like that."

"What do you mean it doesn't work like that?" I was genuinely perplexed.

She was, of course, right. I know now that it was a completely unrealistic expectation.

I have to say, looking back, I'm impressed with how well my therapist kept it together at that moment. I'm not sure I would have that level of composure if someone came into my office today with such an outlandish request.

I learned through this experience that thinking I could control my grief and hasten my way through it just further exacerbated it and extended my suffering. It would have been hard, but I do wonder how things would have been different if I had just leaned into the uncertainty of dealing with that grief. I will never know, but if I am ever tasked with coping with grief like that again, I hope I have the courage to embrace it and cope with it more consciously in real-time. Grief happens after all, and there is no grief checklist or effortless way through it. It will feel like it will overtake you, *but you can manage it*, and the more you manage it, the more you can grow through it. You can cope with tough things, and every challenge you have to face helps you learn to cope even more effectively for the next one.

One more point regarding realistic expectations. Often, I have found that we talk to ourselves in really nasty ways. Like tear you down, scorch the earth, say things you wouldn't say to your childhood bully. We usually do this when we are struggling to cope. Let's try to reduce the rudeness (I initially wanted to say let's eliminate the rudeness, but I had to adjust it to be more realistic). We may always be a little rude to ourselves, but let's at least try to keep it to a minimum. In other words, don't speak to yourself in a crummy matter; speak to yourself as you would speak to your best friend. If you wouldn't speak like that to your best friend, then you know you've got to tackle that rudeness. No judgment: I've certainly called myself a name or two, but when we consciously cope, this should only happen on occasion. We must speak to ourselves positively and with encouragement, and when appropriate, assertive firmness.

Part of having realistic expectations is allowing yourself the flexibility to respond to life and all its varied challenges. This is a skill set that you will work on for the rest of your life. It is one not to be perfected, but one to be honed to help others grow their own confidence in their ability to cope. This is not short-term quick fix work. This is lifelong, fully vested work based entirely on supporting you to cope more effectively with this beautifully complex life we share.

PART 2

A New Way to Cope

When we think of coping with something, we often think of the outcome. I coped with the fight with my sister by taking a walk. I coped with that disappointing news by calling a friend and being vulnerable with my feelings. I coped with feeling insecure by having a dance party for one. I coped by numbing. All these concrete, past-tense behaviors come to mind when we talk about coping, but as we have already discussed, coping is not static; it is active.

How did I know that taking a walk helps me get the anger out effectively? How did I know that calling my friend to lament about the latest challenge, chaos, or uncertainty the universe has supplied me with would give me relief? How did I know that there was mystical healing energy associated with a dance party? How did I know I was numbing; did I realize I was numbing when I did it? All these questions hint at the complex dynamic nature of coping, yet we never talk about the process of figuring out how to cope. *Why is that?*

Well, for one, as we have already discussed, we don't have great verbiage for talking about these things. The lack of universal language is a testament to our need to practice talking openly, honestly, and vulnerably about our mental health and how we cope with it. Secondly, these things are difficult to talk about because they are very subjective. Although we have shared experiences, we also have deeply unique individual experiences that need to be honored. In the pages ahead, I am going to ask you to do the following things:

- practice self-compassion and compassion towards others;

- monitor your energy;

- be open to learning from others;

- feel ALL your feelings;

- accept and make space for challenging things, especially the *extremely* challenging stuff;

- find ways to make meaning and take meaningful action;

- discover creative ways to capture these lessons;

- and finally find ways new/enjoyable/meaningful/effective ways to encourage yourself to do all these things routinely.

So, what in that whole list of things is objective? *None of them.*

We must find more universal ways to talk about mental health and how we cope AND honor that the answers to how we cope, particularly how we cope most effectively, are within the individual themselves. In other words, the data you need to assess how you cope most effectively is within you. Others can give you feedback on how you are coping, support you in coping, and even help you learn how to cope. Still, it is your responsibility to honor, listen, and respond appropriately to the data within you. *The data no one else has access to.* That is the work I can't do for you; that is your end of this deal. What I can do is help you learn how to consciously cope. I give you the prompts; you set the scenes.

Conscious coping is active, a teeter-totter responding to life's natural ups and downs. When we consciously cope, we are more present, compassionate, intentional, and resilient. The best part is that our ability to manage distress increases because of all these things. Sometimes we can even eliminate or shift the distress into something else, which helps progress us forward on our journey to our best lives. EMBRACE does not tell you how to cope, but it gives you the tools to learn how you cope more effectively.

Let's take a moment to explore what conscious coping in real life can look like. Of course, coping is complex, so in the interest of accessibility, I will start with a simple example of something that most of us cope with without necessarily realizing we are coping with it—your commute to work.

Like many of us, you have a routine, 30-minute commute into the office. The traffic is at best frustrating and at worst rage-inducing. You have found yourself on some days arriving at work agitated, and your commute seeps into the rest of your day. The last time that happened, you had snapped at a peer during a morning meeting, causing further stress and embarrassment. After this incident, you had a firm talk with yourself: this has got to change; I get stressed out enough already at work, I can't afford to start off so out of sorts! You hear yourself and become curious about what you can do to shift this stressed-out, overwhelmed commute into something more comfortable. (No perfect here.) *Boom!* You just engaged yourself.

You revisited your previous thought. As you monitored your energy, you knew a tough commute was depleting you before you even started your workday. You realized that you could find ways to increase the chillness of your morning commute, as currently, you are wasting your energy by screaming at the yellow Honda who just cut you off. You realize you have never really paid attention to how angry you get when you drive, but now that you are, you notice that you get really angry. *Really, really angry,* in fact. You say things to people one lane over that you would never say to someone in person.

You reflect upon it, and the term "road rage" comes to mind. It rings wrong in your gut. It's not road rage, you think; it's *work rage.* You realize it's not really about the commute; it's about the anger you have towards your destination. Your boss is a real sack of sugar, and the new VP seems to think micromanaging is always the best approach. As you really reflect on it, you realize that this job has been grating at you for a while, but you've been avoiding your resume because change is hard. What has been going on is an example of misplaced coping. Once you examined this part of you, it became clear that you weren't coping effectively; thus, restorative action is needed.

You decide to update your resume later that day and stop avoiding the fact that you are burnt out at your job. You also decide that in the interim, while you are looking for a new job, you are going to do everything within your power to make your commute as chill as possible. After all, you've identified that you need to rest and recharge so you can show up with energy to cope with the challenging day ahead at a wrong-fit job that depletes you.

The next morning, you get up ten minutes earlier than usual, make yourself a nice to-go coffee, take a moment outside to take a deep breath in, and mindfully take in the world around you and express gratitude. When you get in your car, you switch off your usual political podcast and instead turn on classical music. You visualize yourself having a safe, non-stressed drive. You take some intentional deep breaths and drive away to the best commute of your life (so far!). Sure, there were some moments when your old patterns started to get the best of you, like when the Mustang in front of you seemed to be oblivious to the existence of turn signals. Still, you caught yourself and reminded yourself compassionately about the most realistic expectation. *We don't change overnight.* Real progress, the type you want, is often two steps forward, one step back. Not to worry, that is still progress. You may have enjoyed the best commute of your life so far, but if you keep working on these skills, there will be many more "best commutes."

When you arrive at the office with a new pep in your step, you take another sip of your coffee. As you pack your mug up in your bag, you see what it says on its front: *Be Kind to Your Mind.* You pause and take a moment to absorb this lesson. This morning you focused on being kind to yourself, and it transformed your awful commute into something much more tolerable. You assign meaning to that mug. It is now associated with this hopeful story. In the future, you will smile at it and feel sentimental because of this time. You have made it meaningful to you.

As you walk into your office, your VP looks up from micromanaging someone else and asks if you had a haircut because you look different.

No, you respond, I just had a better commute, and indeed you did. You consciously coped.

As you walk off, you recognize that it was nice that someone else noticed and validated this change for you, *but you did not need that.* You had already done the challenging work of learning from the situation, and by making proactive change, you reduced your suffering. You had done the relieving work of consciously coping, and you are so proud that you have filed this experience away to help you cope with other tough things. Inside, you see it; you make meaning of it all. All they see on the outside is that conscious coping glow.

It is important to point out again that this is a simplified example of what we have to cope with in this world. We would not usually have the luxury of dealing with singular stressors, and solutions are so cut and dry, but from this example, you can see what a difference conscious coping can make in your day-to-day life. It should also be noted that anything can happen when you engage this model. There were no trauma or external issues at play in this initial example. Imagine instead that when you reflected on your feelings of anger, you felt the urge to raise your hands in front of your face to protect yourself. Suddenly you recalled a scary incident from a few years back. It was a one-off; you were sitting in the left turn lane at a red light when a woman approached your passenger door. Before you knew it, she had flung it open and leaned into your car and your space yelling at you for cutting her off, something you did not realize you had done. Before you could respond, she slammed the door and ran back to her van, screeching out as the light turned green. You remember feeling shocked, frozen, thinking, *what just happened?!* This would be an example where trauma has been invited to the party, now you are coping not just what happened in the present, *but also* what happened in the past and how you coped with it. In this case your first step may be to attend therapy (a tool in step A – absorb) to help you integrate your trauma more effectively so that it is less triggering and distressing in the present. You may need to stay at step A – absorb for a while or skip back to step B – brief for a while to learn more about trauma and our physiological response to it. EMBRACE is flexible to whatever path you need to take through it.

Please note that although the steps to EMBRACE are presented in a linear model, coping is not an exclusively linear experience. In learning and developing these skills, it makes sense to start with a linear approach to keep things accessible. Still, eventually, part of what will help you become well-versed in conscious coping is that inevitably the process will get jumbled, and things will happen as they happen.

Imagine that you have an intensely emotional conversation with a dear friend about your relationship and some concerns they need you to address because your actions have harmed it. At that moment, you may find yourself being (unexpectedly) briefed first. At that point, you may monitor your energy and mindfully notice that feedback you have just received was an emotional gut-punch and your energy is (unexpectedly) depleted. Because you are paying attention to your energy, you recognize that fully unpacking what happened is not something you have the capacity for in that moment. So instead of just blowing their feedback off, you take steps to consciously cope with it in the short term. First off, you take a moment and paraphrase back to your friend what you heard them say, and you ask for them to adjust or correct as needed. Then (if possible), you ask your friend for some time and space to reflect upon the feedback they have given you. You ask for that so that you can come back to them with a thorough and thoughtful response. You affirm your desire to do this because you genuinely care for your relationship and want to care for it.

Ultimately, you suggest you and your friend get together for coffee to regroup the following week to revisit their feedback. You suggest this length of time because you know you have to deal with a stressful week at work, and you will not have time to fully unpack and process the incident with your friend until the weekend. Although the ideal scenario is that we will cope with things at the moment, that can't always happen. Sometimes, as in cases like this, we must make an intentional and compassionate choice to punt our coping. If possible, I think it is best practice to name a time and place to revisit conflict. Even if it is tentative, and even if it's just to yourself. In this case that could look like you committing to yourself that you will take some time to journal about this feedback on the weekend when you have more capacity to do so.

So, you gave yourself a conscious break, rest, and recharge, and as soon as you were able to loop back, you did. As you were able to reflect consciously, you realized that your friend had named a pattern of tardiness in how you approached your time with them. *Now that it has been named, it can be tamed.*[5] You recognize that the pattern they have named extends beyond your relationship with them. As you are reflecting, you also notice how much shame you are feeling and are surprised by its intensity. The shame is so intense that you entertain the ultimate escape fantasy for just a moment: you could just ghost your friend and never have to do the challenging work at taking accountability and tending to your relationship with them.

It is tempting. No one enjoys the discomfort of interpersonal conflict, but this is a good friend. The type of friend *that comes and talks to you about things in your relationship that need to change because they are that invested.* Plus, ghosting is never a cute look. Tempted no more, you go back to conscious coping. Once you have reflected, you decide to act by apologizing to your friend and working with them to find restorative action. Additionally, you make a note to ask your therapist for help understanding and dealing with feelings of shame at your next session, as you mindfully noticed how they almost derailed your conscious coping journey.

Finally, you engage with yourself; you give yourself a stern talk about the tardiness. You know promptness is a skill you can work

---

5   Daniel J. Siegel and Tina Payne Bryson, *The Whole-Brain Child: 12 Revolutionary Strategies to Nurture Your Child's Developing Mind* (Delacorte Press, 2011).

on and that your relationships are asking you to do so. You are also compassionate with yourself, recognizing that you've always struggled to be on time, and over time you are making progress, which is so much more important than perfection. You endure by reminding yourself how much you appreciate that you keep showing up to consciously cope with all the tough things you will face.

In this example, EMBRACE was rearranged and played out more like BCMRAEE. Additionally, throughout this example, different skills were used in overlapping and reinforcing ways. For example, the self-talk you used to help you engage with yourself also supported your endurance. Certainly, not every instance of coping can be tied up with such a nice bow at the end. Let's explore now what it looks like to consciously cope with an ongoing trigger.

I have had the privilege of working with clients struggling with chronic illness and pain. One of my clients, in particular, has been struggling with an undiagnosed chronic illness for an extended period. For years they have been tasked with coping with that which has no name. When dealing with chronic illness and pain, people often struggle with gas-lighting themselves, especially if they don't have the luxury of a diagnosis to name what they are experiencing. This client used to engage in a self-flagellating narrative in which the mere existence of their undiagnosed chronic illness was the ultimate evidence of their lack of worth. *This will be the thing that will make people leave me. They will see I have no value and, as such, won't want to do the hard work necessary to support me in learning to cope with being sick.* These thoughts alone would cause them to spin out and feel unable to cope.

I can understand where this narrative was coming from. As counter-intuitive as it sounds, this client's narrative was working to protect them from what really scared them: abandonment. The fear that this would be it, the proverbial straw that broke the client's own family's back. The client was certain they would be unable to cope without their family and erroneously decided that if they were going to be chronically ill, diagnosed or not, they would also, by default, lose their family.

Wait, what?! Yes, that is right, somewhere deep within their unconscious process, the client had decided that they couldn't be sick AND continue to have a healthy, happy family life. When I reflected this to them, they stared back at me and nodded in agreement; after unpacking this, they tentatively agreed that it was possible for them to be both chronically ill AND still have their family. The ineffective coping that the client has been using previously was to catastrophize and plan for the worst-case scenario so that they could try and prepare themselves. When we catastrophize, we believe that if we can predict the worst-case scenario, we will manage it better when the crap hits the fan. In some cases, this is true. In the event of a fire, it is advantageous to know where the exits are, but most of the things we catastrophize are not so cut and dried.

Frankly, catastrophizing is usually a pretty ineffective coping skill. You can stay up all night and think of all the horrifying catastrophes that could happen, and the universe will invariably show up with some new twist to surprise you. Catastrophizing is ineffective (most of the time) because it wastes energy. Similar to avoidance catastrophizing is sometimes the correct tool to cope, but not usually. Many of us overuse it, especially if we aren't paying attention to our coping. That being said, often, people are at least somewhat aware of it. Are you someone who catastrophizes to cope? When has it been effective for you? What has it cost you?

My client's ineffective coping was mutually exclusive to their family. Their transition to conscious coping started with them acknowledging this pattern within themselves. They spoke their intention: to practice leaning into the trust they had for their family and their belief that their family would not just abandon them when the going got rough. The next step was to monitor how this ineffective coping had impacted the client's energy, which was unsurprisingly significant. The client noticed that when they thought about leaning into the trust they have for their family, they felt vulnerable *and* energized. We both agreed that was a good thing and something for them to monitor continually.

The client agreed to talk to their partner directly about their fears to get briefed on what their partner really felt and thought about their chronic illness. The client and I agreed that it would be much better to find out what they really thought and cope with whatever that was, rather than inventing their own narratives.

As we continued to process, the client reported an increasing sense of anxious grief. When I asked them to identify its place and presentation, they said it was climbing up their esophagus, creating a burning sensation. They coughed and became visibly uncomfortable. From there, we were able to work together to understand how past events, experiences, traumas, and triumphs had become knotted together within this difficult-to-cope-with illness. We communed together about the work they needed to do to unravel these things while also celebrating the strength and resilience they had to not only survive up till now but to choose consciously coping, as well. We absorbed this lesson and acknowledged that this would take time and intention to deal with, but there was hope. *There is always hope.*

The client decided to take action and write themselves a letter with their newfound clarity, reminding themselves that their illness was not an indicator of their lack of worth or un-love-ability. Even though the experience was full of challenge, chaos, and uncertainty, those things revealed their strength, courage, and resilience. This letter now lays in the top drawer of their dresser, for whenever they need it. My client tells me that just knowing it is there helps them endure the ongoing daily challenge of coping with an undiagnosed chronic illness. The client also had realistic expectations; they don't expect to wake up one day and be cured, but they do hold themselves accountable to consciously cope, no matter what space it takes up now or in the future. That's some GRADE A conscious coping right there.

CHAPTER 3

What is EMBRACE?

EMBRACE is a mnemonic device that refers to the seven-step framework for conscious coping: ENGAGE, MONITOR, BRIEF, REFLECT, ABSORB, CAPTURE, ENDURE. EMBRACE intends to give you a model for conscious coping that helps to make the abstract world of coping more concrete. I have developed this model through the synthesis of knowledge I have collected throughout my professional experiences, my clinical work, and of course, my own journey to conscious coping. It is an interdisciplinary model developed for the most interdisciplinary subject matter known to us: you.

In the chapters ahead we will dive deeper into each of these seven skills and their associated questions. These questions are broad, and you may be able to answer them immediately or you may need some support to find them, either way at the end of each chapter we will revisit these questions, and I will provide some additional strategies for cultivating your answers. These skills are meant to be used in conjunction with the foundations discussed in the previous section. The key difference between the foundations and the steps of EMBRACE is that you will always be using a growth-focused mindset, validation, resilience to discomfort, radical acceptance, compassion and realistic expectations, regardless of what step you are working on.

ENGAGE — What can I do to support myself in this moment of challenge?

MONITOR — How are my energy levels impacted? What do I need to do for myself to help maintain my energy?

BRIEF — What do I need to learn about this challenge? Who do I need to consult with? What resources can I utilize to help me learn about this challenge?

REFLECT — How do I feel about this challenge? What sense can I make of my feelings?

ABSORB — What do I need to do to consciously cope with this challenge?

CAPTURE — What lesson has this challenge taught me? How can I capture this lesson so that I remember it when I need it?

ENDURE — How can I use the experience of this challenge to help support me in doing the ongoing work required for conscious coping?

Speaking of realistic expectations, let's talk about the elephant in the room. The first question we humans all like to ask is, "Will this 'fix' or 'cure' me?" Here's the bad news. It absolutely does not. The good news is that you do not need a fix; you just need to improve your understanding of and resilience to the challenges you face. It is by no means a silver bullet but a different mindset that allows you to roll with these punches in an empowered manner.

EMBRACE cannot change what is, but it will help you learn how you can consciously cope with the challenges you face, and thus help support you to cope better, which in turn will have you love better, grow better, and yes, even "feel better." EMBRACE is not magic. It requires your ongoing time, intention, and work. It only works if you work it, and working it is one of the best things you can do for your mental health.

The EMBRACE journey is a deep dive into you, your mental health, and how you cope. The journey requires vulnerability, resilience, intention, effort, time, and space. By engaging with yourself, you can hear yourself in a unique way. By encouraging this deep, conscious process work, you can reduce your distress and increase your confidence. EMBRACE is an ongoing investment in yourself. The work may begin with this book, but it does not (and it should not) stop once you have completed it. EMBRACE acts as a reminder of conscious coping in a meaningless world and provides a loose structure for how to do so.

We dive into ourselves because we are curious. Not because we are looking for something to loathe, shame, reject or confirm about ourselves. Being compassionate with ourselves is accepting whatever we find and accepting what is. To the best of our abilities, we work to understand it and learn how to cope with it. We EMBRACE conscious coping as a means of honoring ourselves, our strengths, our journeys.

CHAPTER 4

Engage

The first step towards conscious coping is all about engaging with yourself. In other words, we are talking about the very real and particularly important relationship you have with yourself.

How is your relationship with yourself?

Like our relationships with others, our relationship with ourselves morphs over time. It waxes and wanes; it is influenced by things both internal and external to us. Sometimes we forget about our relationship with ourselves. Without a watchful eye, our imperfect brain can spiral into a cycle of problematic thinking and automatic behaviors: a spiral whose consequences do not just impact you but those around you. Just like in our external relationships, autopilot and apathy tend to be the undoing of our relationship with ourselves.

My relationship with myself was problematic for a long time. I was scared to confront it, to engage with myself in a real way. I once told a therapist that the bully inside me was scarier than any bully I had encountered in real life. I felt hopeless and overwhelmed. It is stunning to think about how much energy I was using just to stay in a problematic relationship with myself. Slowly therapy helped me to imagine how I could use that energy differently. Instead of just using it to control and keep the status quo within me, I could use it to (profoundly) change the circumstances surrounding my relationship with myself.

As I started redirecting my energy away from fighting myself, I invested in more conscious and growth-focused strategies that positively impacted my relationship with myself. The more positive my relationship with myself was, the more clarity I gained on what I needed to do to grow. Over time, it started to change, evolving to what it is today. A (mostly) peaceful relationship with myself, (almost) devoid of meaningless moment-to-moment conflict, where I am confident in my ability to deal with the real struggles all of us face. A work in progress for sure, but a work that is going well, that I enjoy doing. I have learned to accept I will always be working on my relationship with myself, regardless of how well or poorly the process is going.

Self-talk is the epicenter of how I changed my relationship with myself. We talk to ourselves often, and usually, there are a lot of opinions and influences within us that need to be part of the conversation. I have a perfectionist who likes to be really nit-picky, a control freak who wants to argue for power at any juncture, a critic who heckles like no other, a cheerleader who picks me up, lifts me up, and helps me keep going, and a Dateline voice that reminds me constantly that the world is an unsafe place, and that *everywhere* is a great place to be murdered. There are others, but those are the frequent fliers. So why am I here naming all the voices in my head for you? Because what we say about ourselves to ourselves is what we hear. What we hear impacts our ability to cope.

Sometimes we allow one of those voices to dominate the space. My Dateline voice gets obnoxiously loud sometimes, and I have to turn down its volume consciously. I accept what it is trying to tell me and remind myself of my coping power. Yes, the world is an inherently unsafe place that can never be fully predicted, *deep breath in,* but I accept the risk of living and trust in my ability to cope with whatever happens.

I do my best to engage in positive, or at least neutral, self-talk with myself. I do not try to control or stop organic negative self-talk. Intrusive thoughts pop into my mind consistently; this is part of my pathology, something over which I *do not* have control. So, I allow the organic negative self-talk, but I do not let myself reap more of it. Instead, I consciously balance it out.

For example, my critic is currently very loudly (even rudely) saying that it cannot believe I am seriously considering sharing this vulnerable work. What an imposter, what an embarrassment, it snickers at my audacity. My critic would like me to stay home and drink tea.

Okay, so that is just a thought, one that I do not necessarily need to respond to. I gently remind myself.

Instead of engaging my inner critic further, I summon my inner cheerleader and her extra sparkly pom-poms and request her response to the critic.

You can do it, she cheers for me, **it doesn't matter that you don't know it all, what you know is important. SHARE IT! SHARE IT! S-H-A-R-E IT!**

Well, since her pom-poms are so *extra sparkly,* I should probably believe her. *And I do.*

Your ability to cope is impacted by your relationship with yourself, *the quality of which matters*. If you think about it, it is simple: If you do not pay attention to yourself, you will not learn. If you are a jerk to yourself and constantly fighting with yourself, you will have no energy to learn. If you are in denial and avoid learning, there will be nothing to learn. If you do not hold yourself accountable, you will not see lessons when they are presented to you. If you cannot accept what is, you will be unable to learn how things could be.

In general, the recipe for a healthy relationship with yourself starts with the ABCs:

A – Acknowledge your mental health.

B – Believe in your worth, experience, power, and needs.

C – Care for yourself.

Positive and neutral self-talk is an example of how I care for myself. If you can do these things for yourself, you have taken the first step. Congratulations! If, by chance, you struggle with any or all these things, there is no need to fret; included ahead are additional tools to help you cultivate a healthier relationship with yourself.

Acknowledge Your Mental Health

A few years back, I attempted to start a mental health wellness program for businesses; the goal was not just to educate individuals within organizations about mental health and available resources.

Instead, the intent was to get the larger organizations talking about mental health, and by extension, how it impacts their unique eco-systems and cultures. I knew selling new programming would be tough. Still, I was not prepared for the immense denial, avoidance, and resistance I encountered when talking to business stakeholders about the mental health of their organizations.

One CEO told me that their office "didn't talk about such things," and to do so would "undermine the productivity" of the organization (presumably because doing so would value the producer more than the production). Another CFO scoffed at my proposal and questioned why they would be motivated to educate employees about their mental health. Doing so would encourage employees to utilize their health insurance to seek treatment, raising the organization's already high premium costs. I heard a lot of financial reasons for not providing these services. Still, more surprisingly, I heard several downright discriminatory reasons why organizations would not support the work I was attempting to do—from an HR director who stated that they did not "hire people with issues like that" to a director that didn't splice words by saying their organization "did not believe mental health had any role" in a business setting. I was left aghast when an owner of an industrial manufacturing plant stated that their workforce was ~90% male, and since mental health "isn't really an issue for men," there would be no value in bringing in our "touchy-feely mental health stuff."

Okay, yes, on a personal note, it was intense to have people flippantly disregard my profession to my face. Still, more to the point, I was more shocked that these humans actively denied this very real aspect of human nature. What they were saying to me was absurd; mental health and its consequences are everywhere, always, *whether you want to admit it or not.* Unless I am in some type of Blade- Runner-esque future and they were all advanced executive business bots, these people who made these denials just disregarded entire parts of themselves.

All these denials had one thing in common: they tried to distance themselves from the issue at hand. Whether it be for financial, productivity-related, or discriminatory reasons, all of them tossed the hot potato as fast as they could. We have developed an extremely poor strategy of ignoring or devaluing what we do not understand. The thing is that mental health is a very real thing with small and large impacts, and it is for this reason we are currently in the throes of a mental health crisis. We have denied the impact of this part of our lives. Do we need to continue to live in that denial?

We can be radicals by owning, caring for, and celebrating the humanness of our mental health.

Hiding our mental health disempowers us. It communicates to us (and others) that there is shame in our nature. That's totally mucked up! I have mental health, and so do you. So why waste time fighting about its existence? All that does is take energy from us, enegy which is required for us to learn how to accept and cope with our mental health.

Do yourself a favor and stop fighting it. Accept that not only do you have mental health, but you are going to have to work at coping with it for the rest of your life. This is not a badge of failure; it is a badge of realistic flipping expectations!

Believe in Your Worth, Experience, Power, and Needs

There are some fundamental fights we all face within ourselves. Things like questioning our worth or value, the realness and validity of our emotional experience (and resulting needs), and that we have the power to be the expert on ourselves. When we get stuck on questions like, Am I enough? Am I allowed to feel this way? Do I really know best? Is it reasonable to expect people to respect my boundaries? We cannot cope because we are stuck questioning whether we have permission to use our tools. By the way, the answer to all those questions is *always yes*.

Often when people belittle themselves and try to reduce their worth, experience, or power, they put everyone else on a pedestal. I used to do this. Once when I was in grad school, my therapist at the time looked me dead in the eye and very assertively asked me, "What makes you so special that everyone else gets to have worth and you get to have nothing?" She was indignant, and I sat there speechless. Her blunt approach perturbed me, but more than that, I was in awe of her. She had just read me up and down, and when she abruptly asked that question, she challenged my less-than narrative right to its core. She gave me a gift that day; I still use this tool in my own self-talk. On occasion, I have pulled it out in session and confronted my clients in the same way. It is a bold choice, but it is impactful, and when we are talking about dismantling self-defeating patterns of denying our worth, experience, and power, *boldness is needed*.

It was the type of therapy breakthrough moment that simmered within me for days afterward. As I found myself reflecting increasingly on my own worth, I decided to no longer question it. Every human has worth, and they can cope by honoring their status as the only expert on themselves. If that was true for everyone else, it was also true for me, forever and always.

You may be thinking, "But what about evil people?" The elephant in the room for sure. Yes, all people have worth. Even serial killers? Yes, even Ted Bundy himself, but do not get it confused. We don't have to accept, like, or validate other people for them to have these things. People can do terrible things for which there should be consequences, AND all people have worth, their experiences matter, and they are the experts on them. Whether or not they use that expertise and cope in a way that isn't harmful to themselves or others is outside our control.

Moving on from serial killers to more pertinent topics, we all deserve to have boundaries. Our boundaries are our preferred rules of engagement. It is your job to identify, assert, and maintain your boundaries. No one else has a crystal ball to know your boundaries. The only way you can get other people to respect your boundaries is to communicate them. Usually, when we are engaging, we can hear our boundaries, but sometimes we do not know we have a boundary until it has been crossed. At that point, you need to communicate it as clearly as possible and promptly. You must also kindly but firmly reassert that boundary as needed. Boundaries are important; I have found that well-maintained boundaries at the beginning of a relationship are the best prevention. It is like the bowling bumper lanes of coping. If you have them in place, it is a lot harder to spin out. We cannot respect our boundaries if we do not acknowledge or speak to them. Unfortunately, we are not always empowered to recognize and respect our boundaries. If you find yourself in this circumstance, please reach out for help and support. You are a human deserving of your own boundaries. Of course, if we want other people to respect our boundaries, we also must respect theirs. Even if we don't like them or "get them," as long as they aren't hurting us and presumably not hurting the other party or anyone else, it is your job to respect other people's boundaries. If you don't know them and violate them, don't beat yourself up. Once you learn them, the expectation is that you respect them, initiate communication, and undertake restorative action if you violate them in the future.

Deeply related to your boundaries are your expectations. You have permission to have reasonable and flexible expectations. Your expectations are your intentions for what you want out of something. You have wants; you have needs. If you pretend that you don't or that yours don't matter, *stop*. No amount of self-effacing will get you closer to your goals. On the other hand, recognize that not every want, or even need, that you have will be met the ideal way. This is part of the tension we deal with when we consciously cope. We work with what we have, AND we are grateful for what we get.

Care for Yourself

Part of caring for yourself is practicing self-compassion. When you consciously cope, you learn to embrace a proactive and compassionate relationship with yourself and your world. That means accepting yourself as inherently imperfect. This is a lesson I think we all learn across our lifespans.

One day in second grade, I was in my elementary school library when I stumbled upon an intriguing book. It was entitled *Be a Perfect Person in Just Three Days!* Although I was a voracious reader, I remember staring at it and thinking that this book must have some crucial information in it. It was one of the longer chapter books I had picked up at the time, and although I was intimidated by its length, I decided the subject matter was important enough to be worth the investment. I checked it out that day. Excited to learn the secrets of being a perfect person, I cracked it open and dove right in as soon as I was on the bus ride home.

I do not remember all the specifics of the book 30 years on, but here is what I do remember. Every chapter gave some vague information about being a good person, i.e., be kind, honest, etc. The end of each chapter would have a teaser like, *Stay tuned to find out the secret to being a perfect person.*

By the time I got to the last chapter, my eyes bloodshot from near-constant reading for two days straight, I was salivating to know the secret to being a perfect person. However, as I flipped to the last chapter, I noticed it was suspiciously thin. A few brief pages were left, and I *still* did not know the secrets this book promised to share. Nevertheless, I was thrilled to finally learn the secrets this book promised. Well, the whole thing was a gosh dang bait and switch. The last chapter simply said that *perfect people sit in a room and sip tea all day because that is all that perfect people can do.* In other words, there is, of course, no perfect person, and if such a perfect person even did exist, they would be limited to the most mundane life as not to interrupt their perfection. So, unless you really love earl grey tea, *stop trying to be perfect.*

I was livid.

Clearly, that book made its mark on me. I still think about it to this day. While this story still gets me a bit irked, it has become an important reflection point for me. I certainly do more (and want more) in my life than just sitting and sipping tea, which means I must give up the desire to be perfect. Of course, I desire to be perfect, but I also desire to live my life doing something other than sipping chamomile. If that is the case, I must accept my imperfect nature, hold myself to a realistic standard, and compassionately acknowledge the challenge and suffering I (and you) face every day just to show up to life.

As author Stephen Manes so brilliantly explains in this

challenging book from my childhood, "You know what perfect is? Perfect is not eating or drinking or talking or moving a muscle or making even the teensiest mistake. Perfect is never doing anything wrong — which means never doing anything at all. Perfect is boring! So, you're not perfect! Wonderful! Have fun! Eat things that give you bad breath! Trip over your own shoelaces! Laugh! Let somebody else laugh at you! Perfect people never do any of those things. All they do is sit around and sip weak tea and think about how perfect they are."[6] When it comes to your relationship with yourself, do yourself a favor and ditch your perfectionist. They get in the way of your having a healthy relationship with yourself. If you still need an outlet for your perfectionism, take up a detail-oriented hobby, color mandalas, build miniatures, play fantasy football, prune a bonsai, give your perfectionist the fix it craves in small intentional doses.

Routine Self-Care

The conversation around self-care can be confusing. I mean, what is self-care really? The internet seems to point clearly to the path of smoothies, yoga, and facemasks, which, to be fair, are all amazing self-care tools. But there are other forms of self-care, forms that cannot be commodified. Self-care is like the base maintenance plan. All the other things we have discussed are the tactics you use to keep your performance up. On the other hand, self-care is the basic maintenance required for the machine to run. It is your oil change, per se.

---

6   Stephen Manes, *Be a Perfect Person in Just Three Days!* (Cadwallader and Stern, 2018).

I have a memory of a recent moment in my kitchen. I stood exhausted and irritated with my coffee in hand. I was making my mother toast and willing myself to have an appetite. I knew I had not been eating well, and when I had that thought, I immediately realized that there were piles of mail around me, I had not brushed my teeth that morning, and my bedroom looked like a 13-year-old's. As I acknowledged each piece of the puzzle, the black squiggle of apprehension vibrating in my belly rapidly grew. I knew my self-care had been lacking. It was a moment when I saw that I was on the mild end of not taking care of myself, which is the exact right time to intervene. Truthfully, it is always the right time to intervene with our mental health. While the occasional face mask and restorative yoga class are all tools I use from time to time, when I think about my own self-care, I think about the day-to-day stuff—the unsexy things. Connection, movement, diverse intuitive eating, emotional self-check, gratitude, proactive sprucing and straightening up, personal hygiene, medication/vitamin compliance, and laughter are the things that make up my basic maintenance plan. These are the things I need to do every day (or multiple times a day) to keep the engine running.

We need routine and structure in our life. Not crazy inflexible rules, but structures that give us context for how we engage in life are hugely helpful in our journey to coping. The key to good structure is that it must be realistic, and when possible, designed by the individual who will be using it. The structure should keep us feeling safe and secure, but it should not make us feel compressed or overwhelmed.

What I find helpful about thinking about self-care in a tiered way is that it gives me a plan for those weeks when I *can't even*. I have created a baseline self-care plan that requires as little as 15 minutes a day (for me, the goal is just to do it, not to stress about how long I need to do something). If I can keep doing these things every day, I stay in a space to consciously cope. It is a simple concept. The complexity is in the execution of it. I also have an ideal week self-care plan which about once a month I can fully stick to. Yes, my self-care is also a work in progress, but I am compassionate with myself. It is challenging to build and maintain a self-care routine in our hectic, overwhelming and demanding world. If the baseline plan is all I can manage, *I still celebrate*, because why wouldn't I? Taking care of our mental health is challenge, and anyone who does it deserves a confetti canon.

Disengagement

Now that we have explored what it looks like when you engage with yourself, we need to discuss the alternative choice you have regarding your relationship with yourself: Disengagement. The opposite of being engaged with yourself is being disengaged. When we are disengaged, we invalidate, ignore, fight, or even denigrate our mental health. When you are disengaged from your mental health, you cannot manage your energy in such a way that supports your ability to consciously cope. Also, as a bonus, when you are disengaged, you cause great damage to your relationship with yourself. Damage that you can heal, but damage, nonetheless. Typically, you also damage your external relationships and incur additional or exacerbated pre-existing distress.

You do not have to engage with yourself. You can disengage. *You have a choice.* It takes energy to take care of yourself. I will argue all day long that doing so is energy well invested. However, I certainly understand why people have the urge not to invest the energy in conscious coping in the short term. Especially if they already feel depleted. It certainly takes less energy at the beginning to disengage.

Over time though, it will take more from you to disengage than it would have if you had just engaged in the first place. As such, disengaging is usually a losing bet.

My most recent experience of disengaging lasted six months and was in many ways the scariest one. It was not the direct result of the ominous clouds of pathology or trauma. It certainly could not be blamed on a lack of knowledge since I had been a practicing clinician for five-plus years at that point. Instead, it was due to a positive stressor in my life – starting my business. The overwhelm resulting from chasing my dream had me feeling big feelings; at least, I would have been feeling them if I hadn't been invalidating them. The scariest part of this most recent experience is that the cause lies in the fact that I simply allowed myself to stop taking care of myself. I do not think it was a fully conscious choice. However, looking back on it, I think I had some insight into the fact that something problematic was happening to me. Most concerningly, I chose to ignore those insights, a real-life reenactment of the "this is fine" meme of a dog sitting in a burning room.

You may be wondering how something positive could be a trigger. Positive things, just as well as negative things, take energy to cope with. Also, ask anyone who has ever started their own business. There is a lot of great to it, but it is not all butterflies and bank; it is a mixed bag of highs and lows. I decided to return to therapy about six months after starting my business. I am not super proud to admit this, but it took a lot of coaxing. My husband had gently suggested that "perhaps it was time to go back to therapy." There had been much angst, overwhelm, and general gnashing of teeth permeating from my psyche. I was miserable but doing my dang best to act like *everything was okay!*

I got this feedback from him for three months. During these three months, I gave every excuse in the book for not going back. I'm managing it on my own! It is hard to find a good therapist's therapist,

Health insurance! Ugh! Or, my personal favorite, I should go to therapy?! I think you should go to therapy! It did not matter the situation; I had excuses ad nauseam. All the excuses were just covers for what I was really thinking. Oh gosh, I must go back to therapy. I will have to face what I am feeling eventually, and I am not even sure what I am feeling anymore! I would think to myself with alarm, followed up by an even scarier question: What does it mean if a therapist isn't feeling anything?!

It turns out all it meant was that I am human. It is worth noting here that, in retrospect, I am so thankful to have a partner to give me the caring feedback that I needed to go back to treatment. Going back to therapy put me on the path to re-engaging myself and my mental health. It was a gift I gave myself, a hard-fought, difficult-to embrace, beautiful gift, and I do not think I would have done it if I were not reminded that I had the permission and support.

The thing about therapy, and the thing that I wish we talked about more, is the absolute importance of your relationship with the therapist. Without an honest, real, and accessible relationship with your therapist, you cannot reap the benefits of it. I always ask first-time clients who are new to therapy what they expect from this process. Most of the time, they look at me befuddled and state plainly that we "will talk about things?" This is correct, but that is not the magic. Many times, people have already been talking about these things with others. They seem puzzled to be in this room paying for a solution that, on paper at least, has not historically helped—which is why it is important to bring it up.

While we do talk about things—it is called talk therapy, after all—we talk about things *differently* than you would your friends, family, colleague, or the random Joe you meet at the local watering hole. We talk about them differently *because* we have different relationships. We work hard on both sides in therapy to build effective therapeutic alliances that allow us to challenge each other safely and healthily. This relationship dynamic supports the client in building effective insights in themselves that can elicit long-term change. It is an art as much as it is a science, and I will toot my profession's horn for a minute here; it is demanding, life-changing work which is often misunderstood and not valued the way it should be.

One of the biggest barriers for me was knowing that building this type of relationship is a challenging, vulnerable, and time-involved process. I also know that what I need in therapy is someone who will challenge me to feel the heaviness I often default to pushing away instead of dealing with. To support me in being compassionate with myself through their own compassion. And, most importantly, to laugh with me when I need it.

On top of all this, finding *a therapist's therapist* is a bit more of a challenge. I personally love to work with other providers, but it is challenging work. We already "know" the tools, but we still need them reflected to us. And we can be resistant as everyone else. Yes, we know the tools and the science behind what we are doing, but we lack the ability to step outside ourselves and see what an external party can. That is okay; that is just being human. We, as therapists, are a lot of things, but we are not super-human. Even though sometimes we will judge ourselves and think we *should be able to fix* ourselves, this is a myth that does not stand up to inspection.

Finally, one bleak January morning, I awoke exhausted, overwhelmed, and positive that I had totally fudged my life up by pursuing my dreams. I was distressed enough to finally pick up the phone and call my insurance company to get a list of in-network providers. It only took 20 minutes to find a therapist and get scheduled. The barriers I had feared had not presented after all. I felt relieved to have a date to look forward to, a warm compress wrapped around my weary shoulders. I found myself seated on a stiff brocade couch across from my new therapist a few days later. I didn't know it then, but this was my first step towards conscious coping.

If you have experienced something that has required you to disengage to cope, I hope you can permit yourself to seek professional support to unpack this experience. From my own firsthand experiences, I can tell you that traumas, when unacknowledged, tend to stay within us, insidiously shifting how we view ourselves and our world. On the other hand, undealt with traumas keep us running. Whatever happened, you can be still with it, cope with it, and support is out there for you. *All you need to do is reach out.*

Engaging with yourself, just like conscious coping, is a choice you have to make every day. And, to be honest, there will be days when you don't make these choices. That's okay, but the longer you don't make that choice, the harder it will be to change that pattern into the future. If you do not engage with yourself, you will be unable to consciously cope, so do yourself a favor and get back on the conscious coping bandwagon! *I have a tambourine with your name on it!*

Key Question: What can I do to support myself in this moment of challenge?

Ways to cultivate the answer: In general, the best way to get this information is to allow yourself to slow down enough to ask and listen to yourself. The following practices can help:

- Stop what you are doing

- Take a deep breath

- Sit down

- Drink some water

- Change your location

- Find some quiet

- Ask yourself and *trust* whatever answer you get

CHAPTER 5

Monitor

"The energy of the mind is the essence of life."
—ARISTOTLE

You need energy to care for yourself. You need energy to care for others. You need energy to care for your home and community. You need energy, AND your energy is finite. Infinite energy is a fantasy. Because it is finite, it needs to be monitored. Monitoring and maintaining your energy is part of taking care of your mental health and consciously coping. We monitor our mental health by paying attention to our feelings *and* energy levels. We maintain our energy by routinely refueling *and* taking appropriate, preventative action. We prioritize refueling with sources that give us more energy than they cost us.

When we consciously monitor and maintain our energy, we have energy ready to cope effectively *whenever* the need arises. However, when we do not pay attention to our energy, or care for the structures that support it, we struggle to have energy left over to cope effectively. And as you know, when we cope ineffectively, our mental health suffers.

You know best what gives you energy and what takes energy from you. You are also the only one who can accurately assess the

costs vs. benefits of your energy investments. To access this information, you need to be engaged with yourself. Then, when you have
this information, you can consciously manage how you spend your
energy. I find that the more conscious I am with my energy, the more
fluidly I can cope.

Energy is a qualitative experience. It is hard to pin down exactly
what energy is, but you know in your bones when you have energy
and when you do not. When you start paying attention to your
energy levels, you will become more aware of what high and low
energy levels feel like in your mind and body. Higher energy levels
tend to lead to motivation and action; lower levels tend to lead to a
need for resting and recharging.

When I first started monitoring my energy, I developed a quick
gauge of my energy levels—how I responded to phone calls from
friends or family. The phone is just something that takes more
energy from me than other types of interactions, I am not sure why
that is, but I have heard from others that I am not alone. If I feel like
my energy levels are high, I am more likely to answer the phone. If
my levels are low, I am less likely to answer. Usually, it goes something like this. I pick up the phone, sigh, and say sorry, I cannot do
this right now. That is a yellow flag for low energy. If I answer on the
first ring without hesitation, that is a green flag for high energy.

There are many analogies we can use to help us understand our
energy and the crucial effect it has on our functioning, but the one I
like best is to think of ourselves as a car. A car is a machine that needs
an essential ingredient (gas) to run. Without gas, the car cannot run,
and consciously refueling the car is part of how you care for it. When
you start to run out of gas, a warning light appears, signaling to you
that without refueling, your car will soon stall. *If only humans had such
a light!* However, we do have signs for when we are starting to run out

of fuel. Each person has their own signs, but in general, shutting down, fatigue, exhaustion, ineffective coping, numbing or emotional dysregulation can be signs that our energy is running low or is depleted.

How Do You Monitor Your Energy Levels?

Your body and behavior will give you signals about your energy. It is your job to notice and interpret them. I talk to myself in terms of red, yellow, and green flags. Red flags signify I am not coping effectively, and intervention is needed. Yellow flags are a prompt to be curious and check in with myself. I have learned that I am not engaging in a healthy relationship with myself when I ignore red and yellow flags. Green flags are a prod to celebrate how great I am at coping; it is, after all, just as important to look out for the effective as it is the ineffective. If, for whatever reason, I have stopped coping effectively, I can usually look back and acknowledge the many red and yellow flags I saw but chose to ignore.

A big red flag for me is when I have the urge to stay in bed all day and sleep the time away. When this happens, I know my energy is depleted. Sleep is part of how I care for myself, but too much sleep becomes detrimental. Part of my conscious coping is managing the pendulum swings between extremes. I have learned that I need a solid seven to nine hours. I have learned to be curious when I am sleeping more or less than seven to nine hours consistently. Lack of sleep makes me raw. When I am raw, I am more likely to be reactive, heartless, and ineffective. It is ridiculously hard to cope effectively when you are exhausted. That is not a reason not to try.

A yellow flag for me is experiencing feelings of overwhelm. We forget that overwhelm is a feeling. I usually feel overwhelmed when I feel more than one feeling at a time. If you are unable to recognize what you feel, it is easy to get overwhelmed. Overwhelm can yield me ineffective, reactive, and irritable. I have learned when I am overwhelmed to stop and take stock of what I am experiencing. Taking time to unpack what is happening to me emotionally at that moment can provide some immediate relief to the overwhelm. I have learned that overwhelm needs immediate attention when it is identified. When it is not dealt with, it can lead to poor and reactive decision-making and additional distress.

A green flag for me is moments of spontaneous gratitude. Beautifully organic moments where I raise my head to the sky to thank the universe for the pure beauty of the moment I am experiencing in this life. When I get these, I know I am on the right track and am coping consciously. Keep an eye out for these moments; we only get glimpses of them, and if we aren't paying attention or aren't present, we will miss out on them. You work too hard in life to miss out on these. Pay attention, and these glimpses of triumph will present themselves. Practicing gratitude or keeping a gratitude journal can help prompt you to find those moments, for many it can be a self-care practice that is low investment with a high return.

An alternative to the flag method described above is to scale your energy. A dear friend of mine wakes up every day and assesses her energy levels on a -2 - +2 scale. She knew she was depressed when she woke up every day for weeks at a -2, and she knew her medications started to work when several weeks after starting them, she was routinely waking up with a slight improvement at a -1 instead. That little bit of extra lift helped her have enough energy to shower, clean her space, make herself healthful, nutritious, and delicious food. Slowly by doing those things consistently, she started waking up at 0, or neutral. When you are neutral, you might not have all the energy in the world, but you feel equipped to cope effectively with the day ahead. She had a sense of not starting the day at a deficiency. These positive changes all converged to create more positive change for her, and although she is still challenged, she is out there effectively coping with it all, digging into the tough stuff and flaunting that conscious coping vibe. When she started paying attention to her energy, she was able to get clarity and invest in behaviors that cultivated more energy for her.

Both approaches entail a structured (or at least semi-structured) method towards monitoring your energy levels. There is another approach, the completely qualitative method I discussed earlier; just paying attention to your energy and noting it internally within yourself is a less formal way to complete this task. Just find a way to gauge your energy and *do that*. You can refine it as you need to; the most important thing here is that you check in with your energy levels multiple times a day. Everything else can flex.

How Do You Maintain Your Energy?

As humans, we are apt to believe that we have infinite energy because we do not have a concrete gauge for our tank. If we all had gauges that would ding at us when we were running on fumes, we would pay our energy, and its finite nature, more attention. Yet, in our world, we are encouraged, rewarded, even glorified for pushing ourselves past our limits. We must start thinking about our energy differently, more *consciously*.

Part of monitoring is making sure you refuel as needed. Unfortunately, since we do not have a gauge to show us when we need to refuel, it can be hard to remember to do it. For that reason, we should plan to refuel regularly and consistently. To achieve this, I schedule my refuel time. Yes, I put it on the books. It makes it real.

Invest Your Energy Wisely

In addition to paying attention to our energy, we should also be engaging in an ongoing cost/benefit analysis of how our energy is gained, spent, and distributed. We can do this formally by tracking our energy levels and, if helpful, our mood. If you are interested in adopting a formal approach such as this, there are many apps that can help you do so. You can also track your energy levels informally just by checking in with yourself to inquire how much energy you give and receive from all the things in your sphere that require energy. Which by the way is everything.

This does not mean you have to have an aggressive gain on every investment. In fact, I have some investments that tend to take more from me than they give me, but because of love, loyalty, conviction, or *any* other reason, I consciously continue to invest in them. Even though it does not make sense, some things in my life take more from me, and I plan to continue investing in them because I want to.

I *consciously* made that choice. That is the key difference.

Relationships are tricky to evaluate in this way, but nonetheless, we must do so. I'm not saying you should cut off anyone that takes more from you than they give you. *Real talk,* none of us would have families if we did that. No, I'm saying we should at least be conscious enough to say this relationship takes a bit more from me than it gives me. If you can adjust it to balance out better, do so; otherwise, it's okay to say this relationship is worth some of my energy. Again, it is the intention of paying attention and making a conscious decision, whatever it is, that makes all the difference.

Keep An Eye Out for Leaky Pipes

In general, beware of things that waste your energy. When we have a pattern of poor investment, like being rude to ourselves, continuing to engage in toxic relationships, or obsessively trying to change things outside our control, we are wasting our *precious* energy. When we waste our own energy, we have a leaky pipe. The longer our pipes leak, the more energy they let out and the harder they are to repair.

We've already identified a few leaky pipes in the pages prior. Trying to control things outside our control, judging our mental health challenges or the challenges of others, invalidating, avoiding, or demeaning our mental health, lying to our therapists, and lying to ourselves are all ways we can waste our energy. How many of these do you do? How many did you do today? In the last hour? Yeah, we all have them; they are plentiful. Leaky pipes are part of the human experience. It is your job to find and repair the leaky pipes within you. If something exhausted or drains you as soon as you encounter it, be curious about it. I have found that that is usually a yellow flag for leaky pipes.

Hold a Proactive Stance

Finally, part of maintaining your energy is by upholding what I call a proactive stance. When you are proactive, you are neither reactive nor non-reactive, more like a balance of the two. You are prone to react when needed but disciplined enough to practice non-reactivity when it is appropriate to do so. A proactive stance is so important because of three uncomfortable truths:

- If you react to everything, you will have no energy to react when needed.

- If you under-react to everything, you become numb and unable to react when needed.

- If you waste your energy being a jerk to yourself (or any other poor investment), you won't have the energy needed to consciously cope.

A proactive stance gives you the most agility when it comes to preparing for the next challenge you will have to cope with. A proactive stance can also prevent you from spinning out on past events and challenges. When we focus on being proactive, we are forced to be mindful. We are unable to consciously cope if we aren't paying attention to the present.

Your energy, and how you monitor and maintain it, is essential to your ability to cope effectively. Your energy is a precious resource. Self-care can support you in generating more, but that takes energy as well. You must be getting the energy you need to continue to give that energy to others.

When you pay attention to your energy, you unlock a key metric to gauge how you are coping. Of course, there will be highs and lows in the days ahead, days where you are depleted, days when you are buzzing, but when we cope effectively, we learn how to better manage our energy so that we can surf the wild ride of the challenges ahead.

Key Question: How are my energy levels? Do I feel depleted, energized, up AND down, or unsure?

Ways to cultivate the answer:

- Take a moment and do a body scan. A body scan is a meditation wherein you mindfully assess each part of your body and the sensations you are feeling. This technique can help you identify your energy levels; just be conscious when you check in with each part of your body, compassionately asking it for how much capacity it has. Then, assess your overall sense of energy based upon your findings. Headspace and Calm are great apps with many meditations, including body scans available with a membership. Alternatively, YouTube is a great source of free body scans.

- Assign your own red, yellow, and green flags in your life. Keep in mind red flags are a definitive sign that you aren't consciously coping, and intervention is needed. Yellow flags are a prompt to be curious and check in with yourself. Green flags are a prompt to celebrate how well you are coping.

- If you are feeling depleted and need a boost have a dance party with yourself. It is the surest energizer I know.

CHAPTER 6

Brief (and debrief)

"Human beings, who are almost unique in having the ability
to learn from the experience of others, are also remarkable
for their apparent disinclination to do so."
—DOUGLAS ADAMS

A big way we learn about ourselves is from others. Like it or not, there is no effective coping without external support and resources. Like everything else, though, you must work to learn what you do not know. Every once in a while, a nugget of knowledge will arrive unprompted on your doors step. Your job is just to receive them when they come unexpectedly, but most of the time, you have to go out, look for them, and ask for them. You are tasked with finding your teachers and your resources and asking for help when you need to. Keep in mind that not everyone who says they are a teacher in your journey actually is; you alone get to decide.

Conversely, it is important always to stay open to new and challenging information, perspectives, and feedback. Even if you disagree, making a point to expose yourself to things outside of your comfort zone can be a lesson unto itself. Finally, lean appropriately into your support system, and express your gratitude to them by encouraging them to lean appropriately into you. Debrief with them, be receptive and responsive to the feedback you receive, and give feedback the way you would want to receive it. It can be uncomfortable to lean into learning from others. Still, it is essential to our development, and, in my opinion, the discomfort of doing so is a fair cost for all the benefits it brings.

Universal Teachers

We are inherently curious. As such, there are many seekers among us. Those that find lessons within their work, experience, or journey can help us learn more about ourselves and our own journeys. We are constantly being taught. Sometimes it is in formalized settings like schools or offices, but it also happens in passing out in the world. Teachers are everywhere, but you must decide whose class you want to take and whose you will pass on. Universal teachers help us to learn the rules of engagement in our lives. They model through their own experiences, ability, or attitude how to fundamentally navigate the complexities of life, and they do so in a non-personal way. In other words, they are your teacher, but you don't have a personal relationship with them.

I'm so lucky to have so many universal teachers, but Brené Brown's work has influenced my journey to conscious coping the most. Reading *The Gifts of Imperfection* was a transformative experience in my life. I remember where I was when I read it. (Summer 2011, on the elliptical at the Northern Kentucky University gym. *Go Norse!*) I can also remember where I was when I finished it (comfy in bed two days later) and how I felt when I read it (affirmed and energized). I have a *deep* relationship with this book, and by extension, its brilliant author.

Brené, through her wisdom as a researcher and educator, not to mention a human, allows herself to be the vessel through which we can learn about tough things. She is the first person who showed me how possible and powerful this approach could be. I want to acknowledge her and her work, as well as the freedom she has given me to write from my full voice. Other than my middle school obsession with the Backstreet Boys, I have never been a super fan of anyone—until I became acquainted with the genius that is Brené Brown.

Somehow, this person I had never met knew all the words I needed to hear at that moment in my life. Her book gave me the strength to assess my relationship with myself and what impact it had been having across my life. She also made me feel like it was okay to be an imperfect person. Her vulnerability helped guide me to my own. Reading this book will always be a meaningful and important milestone in my life.

I have been recommending this book to others for years, and without fail, people thank me for the recommendation after they read it. I have never known anyone not to find this book a powerful read. Over the years, my crew and I have become fangirls of Brené and her work. That is right; it took until I was 30 years old for me to find my fangirl calling. A few years ago, Brené did an online course with Oprah (talk about learning from the GOATs!), and a friend and I scraped together the money and the time to attend. It was a great course, and I enjoyed it a lot. However, I, unfortunately, held myself back from engaging in it fully.

Part of the course was live weekly conversations with Brené; you could log in and chat with her on Sunday nights. I longed to log on, say hi to my hero, and engage her in a human way, but I just could not get myself to do so. It may seem like I was just shy, but it is worth noting here I am not a shy person. *I was a 2015 Sausage Princess*, a role which involved me dancing on a stage with a plate of mixed sausages in front of hundreds of people in a dirndl, and I was *mostly* sober. In other words, I am not shy; I just did not want to be vulnerable with my hero.

The thought of being vulnerable with the person who helped me learn the importance of vulnerability felt like something I couldn't cope with. It makes me sad and a bit embarrassed to admit that I had hidden from my opportunity to engage with her. I thought I would be judged, or be considered a weirdo, for holding her and her work in such high regard. I do not think she really would have thought these things, but even if she did, the cost of robbing myself of the opportunity hurts so much more overall.

I often think back to this missed opportunity and wonder what would have happened if I had allowed myself to be fangirl vulnerable? I do not know, but I do know that I see now, with more clarity than before, that this level of vulnerability is valuable, regardless of the outcome. I do not know if I will ever get the chance to be fangirl vulnerable with Brené again, so instead, I am calling myself out and hollering to the universe that while I missed an opportunity to be vulnerable before, I am creating my own opportunity to be vulnerable now. Brené, if you ever read this: Hey, girl, you are really the bee's knees. Thanks for all the awesomeness you've added to the conversation about mental health. Also, I adored your appearance in the movie Wine Country, you made a joke about boundaries, and everyone laughed AND learned. Bravo!

How is that for the vulnerable?!

That is *fangirl-level* vulnerability.

Intimate Teachers

While universal teachers are ones whose teachings are global, an intimate teacher is someone in your life with whom you have a personal connection. Ideally, teachers are those whose counsel you trust, but we also learn from those we do not trust, respect, or understand. Conscious coping requires us to take in feedback and learn more about ourselves and the world around us. You know someone is a teacher in your life when they get you to hear things differently.

I know it may be annoying that I'm going to go all heart eyes emoji on my husband in the middle of this, but hear me out, he has been my greatest teacher. He believed in me so much that it rubbed off on me. I struggled to be authentic in my relationships for most of my adolescence into adulthood, which is part of the reason I found myself in a pattern of problematic relationships. When I met my husband, it was as if a light inside me clicked on; he made me feel safe and secure enough to try just being myself. He told me he liked me. He validated me and stuck around when stuff got messy. I was, and continue to be, able to be 100% me. His support was transformative. Not only did he tell me he liked what he saw, but I started to like it myself. There are a million other reasons I love him (he's handsome, funny, a good cook, an amazing dad), but it has been the permission to just be me for which I am most grateful.

I do not necessarily believe that our dreams hold special meaning, but I do believe that we can make meaning out of them. A week after meeting my husband, I had a clear and vivid dream about him. We were standing on the edge of a bridge that, for some reason, ended right in the middle of the Ohio River. The Ohio River is not an appealing river. It is deep brown sludge, fast-moving, and not the type of water that could be described as inviting. In my dream, as we walked to the edge, my husband suddenly jumped in. I remember being disgusted and aghast; I could not believe he had jumped into the nasty river. He signaled to me to jump in behind him. I hesitated, but he kept signaling to me. After a few beats, something inside of me shifted; it told me to jump in. I did, and that was the end of the dream.

My gut told me that the meaning of this dream was to jump into my relationship with my husband and *trust it*. That day, I listened to my gut, consciously took my dating profiles down, and went all in. It was the best decision I've ever made. I am not sure how someone else might interpret this dream, but it doesn't matter. It was mine to make meaning of, and I have learned that the meaning I make of things needs no external validation.

Now let's be clear, we have fought to get here. Literally and figuratively, with others, with each other, and with ourselves. There is no smooth road to authentic relationships. When you are fully vulnerable, you feel every little bump. Intimidating, for sure, but yet the more you hang in there, the more you can commit to the vulnerability of it all, the more you can effectively cope with it. In a healthy relationship, giving and receiving feedback is critical. Tend to your support system and encourage them to tend their own. This is what I mean by debriefing. Talk about what is happening in your relationship with those in the relationship with you. Give feedback in such a way that you would feel as comfortable as possible if you were the one receiving it. Keep in mind not working to improve your relationships does not show love; it shows apathy.

Given the unwieldy nature of relationships and the natural coping challenges they present, I think they are particularly important for us to pay attention to. Meaningful information can be gleaned from the types of relationships we have. Relationships are the most challenging thing we must navigate as humans, and the quality of our relationships has an enormous impact on our mental health. So, what types of relationships do you need to have to support your journey to conscious coping? The best answer to these questions is to look at the best and the worst examples you see in your own life.

Who are Your Relationship Role Models?

Your relationship role models play a vital role in your ability to develop healthy relationships. These are the people that show you how relationships are done well. They don't pretend it's all rainbows and butterflies. Instead, they show up and use their relationships as a tool for their growth. These are the people that show you what success can look like. If you don't know what success looks like, it can be very difficult to orient your relationships for success.

I'm so grateful to have such an excellent example of a relationship in my maternal grandparents, who have been married for over 70 years. They are a fantastic team, and they have fun together. They met as kids, and they have loved each other since then. It has been a beautiful thing to see their relationship, to be born of it. Too few people get the opportunity to see an excellent example of marriage. I am so grateful I was born into a family with a long and successful marriage as its keystone. It is what I hope I can do for my children. To show them that relationships like this are possible and deeply beneficial to the entire family unit. To show them the work we must put into maintaining them and demonstrating the tremendous benefit of doing so. My grandparents gave me this gift; my desire is to regift it to every person I can.

Please do not fret if you cannot think of or don't have relationship role models. The uncomfortable truth is not everyone does. This makes it even more important that we celebrate good relationship role models. It is only through seeing something like marriage done well that we can begin to imagine the potential for such an investment in our own lives. If you need a relationship role model or a fresh example of one, I suggest you inquire with the universe. *Seriously*. Take a moment and set the intention to find more examples, and then (this is the magic) stay open to the opportunities for you to do so. Just remember no relationship is perfect. If you expect it to be, you will be disappointed; if they profess that it is, they are being gratuitous, fraudulent, or don't have the maturity to understand the purely irrational concept of a perfect relationship. Therefore, it's okay to pick and choose. You may have some role models that show both positive things to learn from and negative things that you need to learn vicariously from.

Who are Your Relationship Anti-Role Models?

Okay, real talk, sometimes in life we learn much more from other people's poor examples than we do from their good examples. It's just a human thing, which is why we all love reality TV so dang much. Our anti-role models are the ones who show us what *not to do*. They are the ones that demonstrate poor behaviors and decision-making. Ideally, you learn from these things, so you don't make the same mistakes.

An example of this would be the poor social skills exhibited by the Real Housewives. If you aren't a basic Bravo brat, apologies in advance, as there will be references ahead that may not connect for you. Regardless, the lessons will still be relevant. All you need to know about the Real Housewives is this: it is the same as any reality show ever. The goal is always to get entertaining footage, conflict, and as much sassy drama as you can squeeze out of people. The producers do not want prosocial communication. Prosocial communication does not create TV gold. No one is going to be knocking on my door asking me to be a real housewife because I will attempt not to escalate, but instead compassionately handle the conflict. Now I don't want to put myself *totally* out of the running; if I were invited on as a "friend," it would make for great TV to watch me attempt to talk them down while eating shrimp cocktail.

Now, it is impossible for me, the viewer, to know how much of this behavior is genuine vs. coached, but I will assume that people are at least going to turn it up a notch or two for TV. Why? Because we humans love that crap. We love to see people behaving badly. We like to judge them, chastise them, act as if we are somehow better than them. It is a guilty pleasure many of us share. So, if we are going to continue to delight in the poor examples of how to engage, develop and manage interpersonal relationships, we should at least learn from them. Here are some of the lessons I have learned from The Real Housewives:

Keep your hands to yourself.

- RHONJ S10 Danielle v. Margaret (also do not tell your friends to pull your other friends' fierce ponytail, looking at you, *Teresa.*)

Do not air other people's personal challenges in a public way.

- RHOP S1 Ashley v. Robin & Juan (Just because someone's bankruptcy is public record does not mean it is up for discussion.)

Do not neglect to consider other people's boundaries and safety.

- RHONY S7 LuAnne v. Everyone (Stop being so, like, *uncool.*)

Do not demean others by saying that you are better than someone else.

- RHONY S3 Kelly v. Bethanny (*I am up here*, you're down there.)

Do not be judgmental to other people and things that you do not understand.

- RHOC S1-14 Vicki v. Various (*yuck.*)

Do not fake an illness for attention or other gains.

- RHOC S10 Brooks & Vicki v. Everyone (ugh, *double yuck.*)

Do not manipulate others to start conflict and craft narratives for your gain.

- RHOBH S1-S9 Lisa Vanderpump v. Everyone (sorry, girl, I love you, but your Machiavellian streak is showing.)

Do not spread rumors about people.

- RHOD S2 LeeAnne v. Cary (although, to be honest, visiting "The Round Up" is on my bucket list.)

Do not engage in passive-aggressive gift-giving and regifting.

- RHOBH S7 Kim v. Lisa Rinna (although the fact that the bunny lives in AC's clubhouse is a *splendid example* of meaning-making!)

Do not throw things at others.

- RHONY S6 Aviva v. Everyone (throwing your leg is next level!)

Do not say you are being sincere when your actions clearly demonstrate your lack of sincerity.

- RHONY Season1-? Ramona v. Everyone (*in all sincerity*, hearing her say this makes me want to flip a table.)

Do not flip tables.

- RHONJ S1 Teresa v. Danielle (although I do have to express my gratitude that this incident gave us one of the best memes of all time.)

So now, let's do a prosocial skills remix of the Real Housewives. Let's discuss alternative patterns of behaviors that they could have used. That way, we can learn what not to do from them and then leave with some additional ideas of what we could do if we were in a comparable situation.

Keep your hands to yourself.

- If you feel like you cannot keep your hands to yourself, remove yourself from the situation immediately.

Do not air other people's personal challenges in a public way.

- Find a safe, non-threatening environment to discuss sensitive subjects with others.
- *Do not bring a film crew.*

Do not forget to consider other people's feelings of safety and comfort.

- When you are on vacation with others and have a nighttime visitor, traveling to the other party's residence is more polite than bringing the person to stay in the house with others who may feel unsafe waking up to a topless stranger scrambling eggs in the kitchen. It does not matter how hot they are; behavior like this is the definition of *uncool.*

Do not demean others by saying that you are better than someone else.

- Remember, we are all on the same level. *All of us.*

Do not be judgmental of other people and things you do not understand.

- You do not need to yuck other people's yum.

Do not fake an illness for attention or other gains

- Seriously, this is a concerning behavior. If you think this is happening, it is time to ask for help and/or professional support.

Do not manipulate others to start conflict and craft narratives for your agenda.

- There is more than enough drama in life to go around; think twice before stirring up the drama of your own making.

Do not spread rumors about people.

- Even if your friend told you a rumor that your other's friend's husband was being unfaithful, you do not need to go announcing it with others. However, if you are concerned about it, talk to your friend at the center of the rumor.

- Again, *leave the camera crew at home.* Even if you are in a different room, if you are wearing a mic, you are spreading gossip across the airwaves.

Do not engage in passive-aggressive gift-giving and regifting.

- Donate the gift if you do not want it—no need to add another layer of hurt.

Do not throw things at others.

- I honestly do not know what I would do if I were at a party and someone threw their prosthetic leg at me. *Maybe just get another drink?*

- Be compassionate. We've all had a moment where we have gone off the rails. Let's just be thankful ours wasn't captured on camera and destined to be replayed on repeat into the infinite abyss like this particular mess was.

Do not say you are sincere when your actions clearly demonstrate your lack of sincerity.

- Instead, you can try just not saying anything at all. In all sincerity, your silence is better than any bull you may spew.

Do not flip tables.

- If you are going to do it, make sure you have finished your meal first. *Better yet,* ask for a doggy bag prior to causing a scene.

- Clean up your mess, please! Just because you went full table flip doesn't mean you shouldn't take the time to clean up after yourself.

- Finally, if someone, or something, gets you angry to this level, I would suggest you bring that concern into therapy. Usually, when you start acting out, there is more to the story than just what is directly in front of you. Be compassionate with yourself AND hold yourself accountable to do better.

As you can see, we can learn meaningful things from poor examples as well a good examples. What is important is that we continue to learn from those around us. Relationships are complex, and the more we can learn about their intricacies, the better we can perform in them. When we consciously cope, we stay open to being briefed and learning from external sources. Although resistance to the occasional lesson is expected, I have found that if I stop listening to my teachers or accepting feedback, that is a red flag. It usually means I am avoiding something and not consciously coping. We need these opportunities to brief (and debrief) with others. These opportunities are not only important steps in how we consciously cope; they are also crucial to building and maintaining your support system, which is another form of mental health hygiene.

Psychoeducation

There is one more type of briefing I want to call out, that is psychoeducation. Psychoeducation is exactly what it sounds like, it is education about our psychology. Now there are lots of people who have opinions on mental health out there, that is not what psychoeducation is. Quality psychoeducation is developed by qualified professionals and is evidenced based when possible.

It used to be that psychoeducation was only available in formulized ways, like groups, usually in conjunction with mental health or substance abuse treatment or family therapy. But we all need psychoeducation, and clearly others agree with me because there is a lot of great psychoeducation just a google away. In addition to google there are other ways to seek it out from self-help books such as this one, to support organizations such as the National Institute of Mental Illness (NAMI), to all therapists who are out there spread the good word of psychoeducation on social media, there are many additional places and resources out there. When you think you are alone in your mental health challenges take a moment to look for additional education about it, learning more is always an acceptable starting point.

Key Question: What do I need to learn about this challenge? Who do I need to consult with? What resources can I utilize to help me learn about this challenge?

Ways to cultivate the answers:

- What is your resistance to this challenge? Your resistance will often lead you to the lesson you need to learn.

- Who do you know who has faced the same or similar challenges? How can you find others who may have faced or are facing the same or similar challenges?

CHAPTER 7

Reflect

"Healthy introspection, without undermining oneself; it is
a rare gift to venture into the unexplored depths of the self,
without delusions or fictions, but with an uncorrupted gaze."
—FRIEDRICH NIETZSCHE

You may not have been taught to listen to yourself. When we reflect, we listen to our whole selves and seek to interpret all the different data, both internal and external, that we process throughout our day. In other words, when you reflect, you are allowing yourself to process (or make sense of) all the stimulus (or data) you have taken in, of which your feelings are one part. We are also mindful of what lenses we wear, and how narratives and patterns impact our interpretations. When we process our feelings, we find ways to sit with them and *learn* from them. As we have previously discussed, you can do this in whatever format works best for you. You won't be surprised to find out that each person has different ways to process. Some people find creative activities help them process; others find that they are best able to process by moving their bodies either through dance or exercise. Some people may use music, either the creation or consumption of it, as part of their process; others may find driving helpful. Walking, puzzles, and doing the dishes are all tasks that help me process. Engaging in hands-on tasks like these sends blood to a different portion of our brain, which allows us to process data differently. I found these are particularly good times to allow my mind to wander.

You've probably noticed my tendency to describe my feelings using visual descriptors. This is a representation of my own emotional processing method and a significant part of my own reflection process—*but not the only part.* As I write, I feel the heavy feeling of tiredness pull at my eyelids, little quarter-pound weights dangling, urging me to pack it all up and go to bed. Your feelings are part of this rich landscape you are crafting. When we reflect, we are looking to connect our internal experience with our external experience as a means of cultivating more knowledge about ourselves. The ultimate goal of reflecting is to find clarity. It is only through reflection that we can start to identify themes and patterns playing out in our lives and begin to gauge what is effective vs. ineffective coping for us. It is only by listening to ourselves that we can know what we need to do to take care of ourselves. If you do not reflect, everything just piles on until you feel a mishmash of things, resulting in burnout. Here is another uncomfortable truth: you only have two choices—process now or process later. There is no "process never" option as avoidance does not work forever unless you totally check out of your life.

Remember, reflection is not always immediate or concise; sometimes, you must sit with things over extended periods and let their messages unfurl. It's okay not to have all the information; sometimes, acknowledging that alone can be meaningful progress, and reflection is a key part of making progress. The four major components of reflection are identifying your feelings, feeling all your feels, trusting your gut, and noticing patterns. Each provides an important role in how you learn from yourself.

Identifying Your Feelings

To process your feelings, you first need to identify them. Before we jump in, it will be helpful to our discussion if we take some time to review the difference between emotions and feelings and how we can categorize our feelings. First off, although we use these words interchangeably, there is a difference between emotions and feelings. Emotions refer to bodily reactions in response to neurotransmitters and hormones released by the brain. On the other hand, feelings are your conscious experience of these emotional reactions. Both factors affect how we experience and reflect upon emotion. The good news is that the more we practice naming our emotions, the more we can connect the sensations associated with the experience of our emotions and the thoughts and reactions that are associated with our feelings.

You won't be surprised to hear me say that a big challenge of identifying our feelings is our lack of language. This is where feeling wheels can be incredibly helpful. Feelings wheels show us the relationships between feelings and the spectrum in which they exist. There are many feelings wheels out there, but I like the one created by Geoffrey Roberts, which I have included below. I like this model because it is so comprehensive (120 feelings!) and makes space for all the feels, not just the popular ones (*I'm looking at you, disillusioned!*).

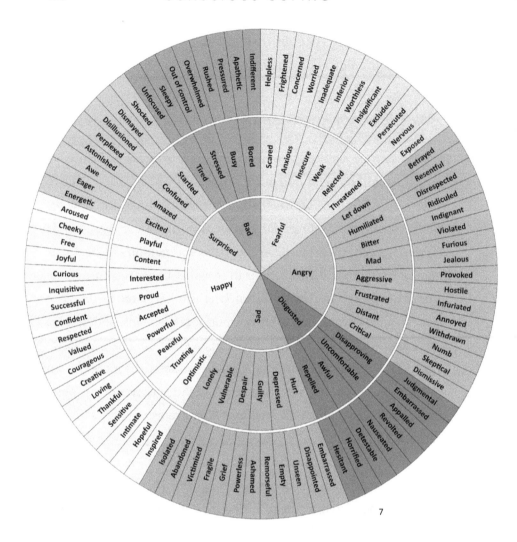

7

Each of these feelings has its own universally understood meaning, as well as the meaning we individually ascribe to it. You and I both understand what it means to feel worried, but only I can identify the wringing sour sensation that fills my stomach and makes me

7   This feeling wheel has been published with permission by the creator Geoffrey Roberts.

nauseous when I feel worried. It is important for you to be familiar with both the shared meaning and personal sensation of emotions. Knowing what sensations you tend to associate with specific feelings is helpful information. Keep an eye out for it.

Feeling All the Feels

It is important for you to feel all the feels. Feeling your feelings *is not a weakness*. Rather, it is an essential act that allows you to access an invaluable barometer for your life. You can be sad, anxious, and grief-stricken while also mentally healthy and consciously coping. There has long been an assumption that something is wrong with experiencing so-called "negative emotions," or even more concerning, the belief that you *should be* happy all the time. An essential part of coping with your mental health is how you attend to, take care of, and react to your emotional experience. If you cannot feel your emotions (or you do not feel a range of emotions), you are not coping effectively. Your feelings do not define the quality of your mental health, but your ability to cope with them does.

Your feelings matter. They aren't just meaningless blips that happen throughout our day; they have immense value and can add great depth and meaning to our lives, but we must allow and respect them. Conversely, not engaging with our feelings causes serious biological, interpersonal, intrapersonal, and community harm. Some may scoff at the sentence above and suggest that this belief is only a figment of my gender, generation, or profession, or label me a "snowflake" with nothing meaningful to say. As much as I disagree with these reactions, all of these are acceptable responses. Why? Because quite frankly, they are all related to feelings. Those responses come from anger, fear, or even confusion. It does not matter if you have a negative emotional response to my argument. Through your response, you have proven my argument to be true: feelings exist, and they matter.

Let us start by laying out a few uncomfortable truths about feelings:

1. Feelings just are. You cannot control your feelings.
2. Feelings are neither good nor bad. They exist on a spectrum of experience; we culturally define what is "good" and "bad."
3. Feelings are transient in nature. We only release them to move on by listening to them and processing them.
4. You cannot pick and choose what feelings you feel. You must feel all the feels. Or you feel none of the feels.
5. Learning to identify, process, and respond to your feelings is part of the ongoing work of learning to consciously cope
6. Feelings are valuable. They are important data and barometers for our mental health and coping.
7. The internal experience of feelings is a qualitative one. You are the only one who has access to the data.
8. We must face and deal with our feelings; in other words, we must cope with them.
9. When we distance ourselves from our feelings, we distance ourselves from our mental health. We use the same strategies for both.
10. Some feelings are more challenging than others and thus need additional monitoring and support.

Feelings are your response to experience. Even though they are abstract, they are full of meaning, but they take work to unpack and understand. Their purpose is to keep us informed and aware of what is happening to us. We cannot control feelings. You cannot make yourself, or anyone else, feel (or not feel) a certain way. We tend to judge our feelings, mostly due to a mistaken belief that they are within our control. Stop trying to control your feelings or the feelings of others. Instead, let us take a non-judgmental approach and view feelings as data.

Have you ever been hangry before? The lovely emotional experience that steams from being so hungry you are angry. This is a fantastic example of a feeling as data. The feeling tells you that you need to eat, you need fuel, and the longer you go without the necessary fuel, the worse your emotional state gets, which communicates the urgency of the message. Additionally, if you are anything like me, your external behaviors will start to communicate the urgency of this feeling and your related need. Fun fact: when my husband and I first met, he said he did not believe that "hangry was a real thing." Not only does he now believe it is real, but he also has great respect for the urgency of hangry and will be the first to validate my feeling when my hanger presents.

Feelings matter because feelings are part of being human. To deny our feelings, or pretend they are valueless and meaningless, is to deny ourselves. When we deny ourselves the right to engage with our feelings, the inherent chaos and challenge of the world around us multiplies exponentially, wearing us down to a point where we start just going through the motions. A robot can just go through the motions; *a human cannot.*

We cannot control our feelings, even though we think that we can, or at least that we should be able to. Feelings just are. Yet, we spend a lot of time trying to talk ourselves out of our feelings. For example, let us say you are upset with a friend for not returning your calls, but you know your friend is having a tough time. So, you might have had the thought that I can't be mad at them. You think you cannot be mad because you empathize with them and their current challenges. The problem is that *you are mad* about it, but you also have compassion for them. If you cannot be mad at them, you cannot talk to them about how you are feeling, which means that you cannot take action and thus cannot address your feeling and resolve it. A more compassionate approach to this would be to say I am hurt and angry because my friend did not return my call, but I know that they are having a tough time, so I will wait to talk to them about it until they have more capacity for us to address and resolve this issue.

The key difference is that you *allow the feeling* and then decide how to address it compassionately. You show compassion for your friend by recognizing their limited capacity AND show compassion for yourself by acknowledging that the hurt and anger you feel need to be addressed. If you do not address these things, the emotions can morph into resentment and contempt, causing further difficulties in the relationship. This is also how we care for our relationships. If we do not vocalize our emotions, needs, or expectations, we do not allow the other person to know what needs to happen for the relationship to continue growing. No matter how amazing they are, they aren't mind readers; you have to communicate how you feel with them. Transparently, assertively, vulnerably—that is how we honor our relationships.

We will also try to change our feelings or even the feelings of those around us. As you know by now, I *love* reality television. People are fascinating to me, and although reality TV presents a highly produced version of humans and their relationships, I still find it to be enthralling (clearly). A common reality TV story arc is people having a conflict over what they think other people *should* or *should not* feel. A totally absurd story arc, as the belief of what we or others should or should not feel is *meaningless*, as feelings are not within our control. Just as feelings are not "good" or "bad," nor are they "right" or "wrong," *they just are.* Certainly, we can associate with our feelings thoughts or behaviors that may be "good or bad" or "right or wrong," but the feelings themselves are not subject to revision. To judge feelings, whether our own or other people's, is to invalidate them.

We tend to think that if we cannot rationally understand someone else's feelings, then there must be something "wrong" with the feeling. Here is a tip: we cannot always rationally understand someone else's feelings, just like we cannot always rationally understand our own. Feelings are not always rational, which does not make them less valuable. Stop trying to control or change your feelings or the feelings of others. It is a leaky pipe.

While we are at it, there is no such thing as a "good" or a "bad" feeling; these are just judgmental descriptors of our emotional states—states that can have a profound impact on our mental health. When I ignore my feelings, I start to default back to glossing them over and making statements like *I feel crappy.* "Crappy" is not a feeling. It is just a quick way of communicating that I am disengaged with my feelings and do not have or cannot be bothered to gather the energy I need to give a flying flip about them. Pay attention to how you communicate your feelings with yourself and others. Doing so will provide you with a great deal of information on how engaged or disengaged you are with your emotional experience. Paying attention to your feelings may sound like a lot of work, but it takes less energy from you in the long run when you do it routinely.

Keep in mind that we all have different emotional experiences. Just because you experience one feeling does not mean that others will feel the same way. We all have different spectrums of feeling our feelings. A few years back, I planned a secret romantic getaway for my husband's birthday. I was so excited for the big reveal, and I envisioned how I would squeal with joy and excitement if I were the recipient of such a gift. Well, the time for the big reveal came, and he reacted with the flat enthusiasm of someone heading out to Jury Duty. I mean, he was clearly intrigued by it, but his emotional experience was not as intense as I thought it *should* be. Long story short, I got bummed out, and awkwardness ensued.

Once the moment had passed, and we unpacked what had happened, we were able to identify the uncomfortable elephant in the room. I had projected onto my husband what I thought his emotional response would be (or what it should be), and he had experienced his emotions less intensely than I would have and thus thought he should have. As such, I had assumed that because he did not have the emotional response I expected, he did not care or appreciate the gift, *which was not true.*

We are different in how we experience our emotions, and in a healthy relationship, we must embrace and honor these differences. You may not experience feelings to the same degree as the human next to you; we all have a different spectrum of our emotional experience, but that should not be misinterpreted as not feeling. We all feel, *but we all feel differently.*

Feelings are valuable to how we take care of our mental health and cope. Often because feelings are challenging, we will treat them as an inconvenience. To be fair, feelings can be inconvenient, but they are never without value. Even when you identify a feeling that is not helpful, it still has value. I often feel guilty when I consciously take time and energy away from other people to care for myself. Our culture has long instituted the idea that self-care is selfish (it is not, it is vital). Self-care is an essential part of how we recharge our energy so that we can continue to give our energy to those around us. Regardless, although I know this rationally, I still feel uncomfortable when I prioritize my self-care.

When I acknowledge that guilt, I know that it is junk data. Often when the guilty feeling looms, it is located on the bottom of my feet, vibrating restless energy that makes it hard to relax. When I listen to this feeling, it tells me that I am doing something wrong and should stop. This feeling and the covert message within it are very much related to toxic, macro messages about self-care. The challenge here is to engage the knowledge within me; the knowledge that knows this type of thought process is baloney. You cannot care for others if you do not care for yourself—another uncomfortable truth.

The rational part of me can help me understand that the feeling is not wrong, but my urge to flee from it is. I know I need to prioritize my self-care; the guilt just underscores my discomfort with doing so, which does not mean I should stop. I know I can effectively cope with it by feeling it and releasing it. Sure, it would be easier just to disregard the feeling, but that would not be productive. To be sure, if I had decided to engage in self-care that was harmful to myself or others, and the guilt I was feeling was related to that, that would require a different response. This is why it is important to interrogate all feelings, even ones that you suspect may be "junk data."

So, if you can get on board with my hypothesis that feelings are data, are you allowing yourself to engage with your emotional data set? Maybe not, and there are a lot of reasons why you may not be. You may not know how to, or you may not see the value of doing so, or you may have such a backlog that you do not know where to start. Whatever your reason may be, today is a new day, and *it is never too late to change how you engage with your mental health or consciously cope with it.*

If feelings are data, you have the power to either choose to capture them or discard them, but you must examine them first. Otherwise, it is not data; it is just noise. Noise that will not go away on its own, which is why we must examine it first. Even when we routinely engage with our emotional data, it can be unwieldy. Feelings are sometimes so ridiculous, unpredictable, or difficult that we will have feelings *about* our feelings, further compounding them. When this happens, we experience a meta-emotion. Meta-emotions can echo powerfully throughout the space and time of our lives.

It is important to note that when we do not allow ourselves to feel our feelings or numb them, it does not stop them. It simply pushes them down, cluttering up your emotional life, increasing your distress, creating unfinished business, overwhelm, and of course, leaky pipes. If you do not feel a feeling and deal with it at that moment, you simply kick the can down the road and create more work for yourself in the future. Sometimes we need to kick the can down the road, but let's be aware of when and how we do that.

Feelings, and your associated experience of comfort and discomfort, are transient in nature, but you must encourage them to release by processing them. We process our feelings by listening to them, receiving their message, and interpreting it. How you go about these things is unique to you. It seems strange to me that we constantly talk about feelings to ourselves and each other while simultaneously disavowing and judging them. I often tell clients, very honestly, that I do not always like feelings myself. They are murky and abstract in nature, take energy to understand and deal with, and sometimes just downright inconvenient. Of course, they can also be lovely and bring true depth and meaning to our lives and relationships, but not without the full scope of feelings and the work required to unpack them can we experience them in this way.

I doubt you will see it as such in the beginning; I know I did not. I remember rolling my eyes at all the therapists who told me I needed to *feel my feelings* versus trying to intellectualize them away. I remember challenging one therapist, gripping his leather couch until my knuckles were white, "But how do I just sit with a feeling?" His only response to my demand was to look up from his clipboard, shrug, and say, "You have to figure that part out on your own." It was deeply dissatisfying then, but I now see it as one of the greatest and most meaningful challenges a therapist has ever given me.

As much as the concept irritated me in its simplicity, something funny happened when I learned how I could sit with my feelings, allow them to be, and manage them in such a way that they brought more value into my life. I stopped running from myself and my feelings. It turns out running from yourself takes a tremendous amount of energy and is highly ineffective because wherever you run, *there you will be.* Instead, I found strength in sitting with myself and the discomfort of feeling my feelings and found myself with the energy to follow other paths I wanted for myself, including becoming a psychotherapist. Make no mistake; this was no quick task—this was the culmination of ten years of work that is still ongoing. It is a commitment I made to myself. While I still stumble at times, I continue to see the value in making this choice every single day.

Example Emotional Process Method

It is important to note that I've adapted the process below to meet my unique needs, but it is a variation of an exercise my current therapist taught me. The steps below help me acknowledge and get more information about how I feel. Feel free to borrow it in its entirety, partially, reinvent it, or replace it with something else. As usual, you are the expert on yourself, so trust yourself that you can learn how to do this—my experience is just a starting point. So, without further ado, I present to you *the box of bees* method.

One of my favorite pro-mental health behaviors is visualization, which is just a fancy way of saying I like to imagine my emotions and challenging situations differently within my mind. I get a different take on what I am experiencing when I let my brain engage in this creative process. It helps me crystallize the qualitative data of what I am experiencing. Although you can do this many different ways, one of the easiest is through a basic set of questions to ask yourself when you are struggling with difficult-to-identify or confusing emotions. Take a minute, get comfortable, and when you are ready, take at least three deep breaths before you ask yourself these questions. These questions may seem strange. That's okay; they aren't meant for your rational mind. They are intended to stimulate more intuitive parts of your brain. Try not to think about your answers too much; just allow whatever answer pops up in your mind to be the correct answer. **There is no right or wrong**. Your main goal is to gain insight into what you are feeling while doing the exercise; interpreting it formally comes later on in the process.

- Where do you feel the emotion in your body?

- What sensation do you feel in your body? (i.e., tight, heavy, tingly, pins and needles, etc.)

- What shape is the emotion?

- What temperature is it?

- Can you touch it, or would your hand go right through it?

- Does it remind you of any type of tangible item?

- If I ask you to remove it from your body, can you do so and hold it in front of you?

- If you cannot remove it, what is preventing you from doing so? What is it trying to tell you?

- If you can remove it, look at it in your hands in front of you. What else do you notice about how it looks?

- What is it trying to tell you?

- Do you think you could put it somewhere safe, for at least a little while, and come back to it when you need it?

- If so, go ahead and visualize doing so.

- Now, where did you put it?

- Why did you put it there?

- If you cannot put it down, what would help you put it down?

I know you may be thinking this sounds wacky. I get it. I wasn't sold at first, but for me, I swear it works, and I know others for whom it works as well. I also know people who are not fans of it, which is fine. As usual, you got to figure out what works for you. This process works for me so well because when I am dealing with something challenging, I can get stuck in it. This approach helps me get more information about what is going on and what else I need to do (if anything) to address it. I also think that visualizing putting it down helps my brain unstick itself from whatever it was stuck on. It is a way to communicate to my brain to say *thank you*; I heard the message; there is nothing more to do about this right now, so let us clear some space for the next challenge to cope with.

My favorite story to demonstrate the power of this practice is when my husband started a new job a few years back. It was incredibly stressful and a big step for him professionally. His new job required him to manage website servers, and it was an area where he felt particularly ill-equipped. One day a few weeks in, the servers went sideways, and he was tasked with managing it on his own for the first time. He came home clearly rattled and anxious. When I took him through this activity, he identified that he visualized him-self carrying a box of bees around with him. He was panicked that he would do something that would cause them to revolt, leading to utter chaos and professional destruction. When he said a box of bees, I immediately connected with the weight of the emotions he was hold-ing. I mean, a box of bees elicits a specific type of terror. Especially when it is in your home. So, we agreed that the box of bees needed to stay outside our house, and since then, he has been able to effectively check the box of bees into our back yard at the end of the workday.

Diving into reflection like this is significant work. As such, there are two additional strategies I would like to impart upon you to be used in connection with the box of bees: grounding and containment. Let's start by exploring grounding. When we ground ourselves, we intentionally quiet our minds and bring ourselves into the present moment. We often need grounding to help us manage the urge to go into the past or the future when experienc-ing intense emotions.

When you are satisfied that you have gathered all the informa-tion you can, come back to this present moment. This is a great time to do a grounding exercise to ensure you are back to being present. There are many grounding practices, but here is one of my favorites.

- Grab an object, any object, nearby. *I grab a pad of Post-its.*

- Notice 3 things about this object. *It's super bright pink; its edges are crinkled up, there are black pen markings on it.*

- Hold on to the object; notice the weight of it. *It is lighter than I thought.*

- Now consciously touch it; what is the texture? *It is rough, and the corners are sharp.*

- Finally, does that object have a smell to it? *I smell the acrid scent of the marker on the page.*
- Bonus question: How can the object help me cope? *I can write myself a self-care reminder note with these Post-it notes.*

Similar to grounding, the practice of containment is meant to help you keep your identified challenges from seeping into other aspects of your life. My husband contained the box of bees by not allowing them into the house. This was an easy choice as there is no world where you would willingly invite a box of bees into your home. Containment can be a place, real or imagined, or a vessel, real or imagined, where you can store your visualization when you are done with it. For me, it is the woods behind my house, what I lovingly refer to as my psychological junkyard. The dense trees hide the secret garden of past hurts, anxieties, and unfinished business. Deep within them, those woods are laden with boulders of past trauma, a quicksand pit of existential anxiety, and memories of college friends whose faces I miss.

A client of mine imagined their containment system was their compost bin. They would mentally unload into it when they went to rotate it daily. When they did, they took a moment to reflect on their intentional choice to release their challenges into the compost to transform them into something better. In this case, *literally.* Their compost also supports their gardening (which is their favorite self-care activity) and their access to healthful food (essential for the key nutrients they need to help their brain cope with the chronic depression they had experienced since childhood). Their compost bin became a coping triple threat! What's that I smell? That's the aroma of conscious coping!

It's not that you have banished these things; on the contrary, you have put them somewhere safe. Somewhere where you can revisit them as needed. It occurred to me that I had a huge falling out with one of those college friends back there, and for nearly 15 years, we haven't talked. I feel the sadness and regret of that at this moment. I don't even remember what we fought about? Perhaps it is time for me to revisit our unfinished business. When we practice containment, we can practice more control over our coping, and when used effectively, we can create a "staging-ground" so that when we have the capacity to return to it, we can. As I reflect on my friend, I realize that I feel differently now about whatever happened. I miss my friend, and it probably took me all this time to see that clearly. Sometimes conscious coping starts by realizing something within you: that something needs some time and attention. I vow to think more about how I can resolve this unfinished business.

I spend a fair amount of my time as a psychotherapist assisting people with this simple yet quite challenging prospect of paying attention to their feelings and working proactively to understand them, all in a bid to cope with them as consciously and effectively as possible. One of the most misleading beliefs about mental health and how to cope with it is that these things should be quickly and easily fixed. Look, first off, you know how I feel about the word "fix," but more to point is that when you reflect, it takes time. It also takes practice to learn how you need to do it. I'm interested in hearing how you do it, and I hope I get to because if we can start talking about these things, we really are changing the conversation about mental health.

Trust Your Gut

Your gut is your guide. If your gut feels unsettled about something, that is usually a red or at least yellow flag. Another term for our gut is intuition, an important and sometimes undervalued sense. Sometimes this intuition directs our behavior, like when you happen to sense a need to move over on the sidewalk right before a cyclist zooms by, narrowly avoiding a nasty accident. Sometimes our intuition kicks in by helping us interpret things in our lives, such as events, themes, and non-verbal communications.

To trust your gut, we must be able to trust ourselves. If you struggle to trust yourself, try making immediate decisions about small things and then sticking by them. Whether it is repainting your bathroom green or blue (blue!), burgers or pizza for dinner (pizza!), or even whether you should stay or go (go!). Whatever the decision, practice not second-guessing it. Lean into the trust you have for yourself—the trust that led you to make the right choice at that moment. The trust that worst case scenario making a mistake will help us figure out how to adjust our course.

Notice Patterns

We all have patterns. Patterns are hard to see from the inside looking out *but trust me*; you have them—we all do. Not all patterns are harmful, but we must do our best to pay attention to our patterns and adjust them when they are unhealthy or problematic for us. Sometimes we have a pattern that was healthy for us for a season of our lives but then become toxic in another season. We gain skills throughout our lives because we need them, the skills when repeatedly reinforced can metastasize as patterns. The thing is though as adaptive beings in a dynamic landscape, patterns can be dangerous, they hold us tethered to what was, which limits what is and could be. Be courageous and notice your patterns and fully evaluate if they still serve you. If they no longer do release them and compassionately remember, that no matter how maladaptive they are now, they served you once.

An example of this I often see is with clients who have experienced early childhood trauma. They are often hypervigilant, paying rapt attention to all the different stimuli and making a conscious plan for how best to protect or defend themselves from any number of real or perceived threats. *They are always on.* Ready to react, most likely because that was the most effective coping skill for them when they were young dealing with a traumatic or unsafe environment. If their job was to just to survive an unsafe or traumatic situation when they were young, they weren't doing anything wrong. In fact, they were coping the best way they could, with the limited resources of a child. We would not judge this child coping this way, it makes perfect sense. The issue is that that pattern will continue into adulthood if not intentionally interrupted. I've seen a lot of adults who experienced childhood trauma and have gone on to live full, successful, meaningful and ultimately safe lives. So, what happens when that hypervigilance presents repeatedly when the original threat has long since dissipated? It can become extremely disruptive. If you are always looking for the exits, you will miss the interiors after all.

Have you ever bought a grab bag? I do not see them very often anymore, but I have vivid memories of them from childhood. Opaque bags packed with mystery purchased for a flat rate. To me, the stuff inside was cool, but it was second fiddle to the intoxicating excitement of buying a mystery bag. I would always buy them with my mother when I was young, and we would share the excitement of revealing the bags' mysteries together.

When I was an undergraduate, I briefly rediscovered grab bags and went through a phase where I became fixated with them. I do not use the term fixation lightly here; my thirst for grab bags was such that it became semi-disruptive to my life. It was about as serious as anything related to grab bags can be.

In my neighborhood, there was a store called DEALS! and it was simple in its promise; there were indeed deals to be found at this store. The name first drew me into the store on a random loaf about college weekend. As I looked around the initially underwhelming bric-a-brac, I was not too impressed, but then I saw in a back corner of the store a simple cardboard sign pointing to a rack of nameless paper bags. "Grab bags $5," the sign read, beckoning me closer. As I stood in front of these brown paper mysteries, I found myself transported back to my childhood. I remembered picking out grab bags with my mother, delighted by the mystique of not knowing what exactly was in the bag. On my first visit, I snatched up two and hurried back to my dorm room to rip them open and behold the treasures within.

I couldn't tell you what was in these bags; indeed, it didn't matter. It was pure fun. I should mention that during this period of my life, I was deep in the inky dark of grief. My father had died only months before, and I was desperate for anything that would distract me from the pit of gloom I had been inhabiting. The DEALS! store and the grab bags they sold became the ray of light I was looking for. They had become a source of adventure and delight for me, and at $5 a pop, the cost was low and the benefit high. *I was hooked.*

Over time my grab bag addiction snowballed. It got to the point that when I was sad, bored, or mad, I would buy a grab bag. I know it must seem silly, but these grab bags started as a unique way to cope during that time. As ridiculous as it seems, there is not much difference neurochemically to what happens when you win big at the casino and find a great deal at a discount store. Your brain interprets that as a win, a score, a feel-good event, and the good-times neurochemicals roll.

The problem with casinos and grab bags is that they offer a fleeting high; once it is gone, you are looking for the next hit. This fixation can lead you to a pattern where you reach for only one tool in your tool kit. When this happens, the tool starts to lose its efficacy, and you forget to practice your other skills. In other words, let us say you use running to cope, and that is all you use. If you get injured and cannot use that tool and do not have other tools ready for you to use, you are at an immediate disadvantage.

My love affair with grab bags went on for a solid six months; who knows how much crap I collected in that time. I can't tell you when it transitioned from something healthy to unhealthy, but I didn't think to question it until one day, without warning, the grab bags disappeared. I went back for weeks, but they never returned. It was an ending to my increasingly problematic grab bag habit. It wasn't all bad. They had given me some fun, adventure, and nostalgia. They connected me back to something I needed, a simpler time, a time when I still had both my parents, a time when I felt safer in the world, a time before I learned about the grab bag nature of life. I grieved their loss, AND simultaneously, part of me knew it was time to move on. What had been healthy was becoming unhealthy. It also helped that the quality of the grab bags was declining; the last one I had gotten was just assorted dental floss, which was pretty disappointing. The writing was on the wall, but I will always have a soft spot for grab bags and the pure joy they have brought me.

Real talk, my brief grab bag fixation was, unfortunately, part of a larger pattern present in that period in my life. After my dad died, I felt so numb for so long I would engage in anything vaguely interesting if it helped me feel again. I did not really care whether something was healthy for me or even really gave it any thought. Instead, I would find something that would give me a spark of something, and I would do it until I could no longer. In this period of my life, numbness ruled. It did not matter if it was grab bags, food, drugs, or alcohol; after all, *the easiest thing to get addicted to is our own brain chemistry.* It is just that grab bags are the cutest version of this story in my life.

Patterns are all around us. Sometimes we know when we are engaging in patterns; often, we do not. Patterns are predictive of outcomes, but not the masters of them. Patterns have rippling impacts, which is why it is so important to do your best to be alert to them. The most dangerous part of patterns is that they lend themselves to automatic behaviors. We learn our patterns by paying attention but also by receiving feedback from others. As a sidebar here: therapy is an excellent tool for identifying and learning about these patterns.

Many of our patterns play out in our relationships; however, the most problematic patterns play out within our relationships with ourselves. Often these patterns are closely tied to narratives we have about ourselves and our world. Patterns and narratives are close cousins, and they can be a mischievous pair. If you are not paying attention, patterns and narratives will take over your life and make everything automatic.

"Patterns" refer to behaviors, "narratives" refer to stories we tell ourselves—often stories that reinforce the pattern and vice versa. Narratives are powerful stories crafted within us that help us make sense of abstract patterns, circumstances, and themes in our lives. They are the stories we tell ourselves that help us make sense of our lives. That is not to suggest that narratives are always positive. Narratives can be helpful just as easily as they can be problematic. A helpful narrative for you in one situation may be unhelpful for you in another. Further, a healthy narrative in one stage of your life may transition to be unhealthy in another. All this is to say we should view narratives with a healthy dose of discernment. Our brains are quite good at telling us what is "true" and "false," but the reality is usually much more nuanced. We need to be mindful that narratives should not become fixed perspectives for seeing the world.

A fixed perspective could be the proverbial rose-colored glasses, but it could also just as easily be poop-colored glasses. For me, an excellent example of an unhelpful narrative is that of the victim. There have certainly been moments in all our lives where we have been victims of circumstances or of others. It is disempowering to be victimized. But the lens of the victim is one that we can put on and take off. This is not to say that your experience did not matter, was not real, or was not important. It is simply to say that as long as you stay in the role of the victim, you are in a disempowered space, unable to tackle the business of consciously coping with the challenge that victimized you. Sometimes we default to the victim lens to avoid the core issue, whatever it is. By staying a victim, we erroneously think we are saving ourselves from the pain of dealing with these experiences. But all we are doing is suspending ourselves within the pain of them.

Dealing with Challenging Feelings

How you cope with excitement is different than how you cope with grief. Why is that? Because, and yes, I know this rhetorical, grief is a different beast that needs additional tools and support when it is presents. It is funny; when I first wrote the story of my young self asking my therapist for a grief checklist, I was very hard on myself. I was ashamed that I came into a therapy session with such unreasonable expectations, and I felt guilty for any distress I may have caused the therapist. This went on for a month. I wouldn't think about it all the time, but the memory of it would pop into my mind, and I would start to cringe with discomfort. Rumination, or getting caught in a thought process, looks like this. It is a yellow flag, one I noticed and promptly ignored. The thing was when I wrote that story down, and when I saw myself through the lens of my current mind, I judged my poor grieving, confused and alone 20-year-old self.

During that month, something funny started to happen. My clients started to come to me and ask for oversimplifications and shortcuts to grief. I was flabbergasted when a long-time client asked if anyone had ever made a grief checklist. As each one of them spoke, unbeknownst to them, *they healed me.* Our shared experience is the antidote to shame, after all. As each of them showed up wanting a shortcut through grief, I was reminded that *I was not alone.* Each instance of their humanness, wishing for something easier than the true challenge of grief, showed me that it wasn't just me. *It was all of us.* I did not judge them; instead, I applauded their courage. They asked for help, after all. Although the details of their questions were different, my answer was always the same: the outcomes of grief come from the journey itself, a challenging, chaotic, and uncertain journey. The more we resist the flow of grief, the more it amplifies. Once again, we have arrived at an uncomfortable truth: shortcuts, quick fixes, and one-size-fits-all options only delay your journey.

I had nothing but compassion for my clients because I saw them as I could not see myself: through my professional lens. Humans just trying to cope the best way they can with things that seem insurmountable. I saw in them what I could not see myself: the genuine wish that grief was easier, more relenting. My experience gave me the answer to their question—no, there is no way around the tide of grief, but I could commune with them in how difficult that was to accept. Yet acceptance of that is an essential, uncomfortable truth. There is no easy way through grief for anyone.

That being said, I think we are better practiced at managing grief than we realize. We primarily only validate "big G" Grief, major grief events like death, separation, significant loss. It is our "little g" grief that we deal with routinely—things like natural endings, transitions, and every day or expected loss. In other words, grief is always around; it's just that we don't always label our grief as such. I think self-judgment gets in the way of us naming all the griefs we regularly encounter.

A while back, we moved from our long-time home in one state over the river to a different state. Despite being in a different state, our new home was six miles away—it was not a major move or relocation. As we got closer to the move, I started to get more and more emotional about it. I was surprised how sad I was to be leaving, but I brushed it off (ineffectively) and just told myself that it was silly to feel that way (check out that blatant invalidation!). Looking back, it just seemed like such a small, *insignificant* thing that I didn't think I should have to grieve, but yet I was. It took months for me to say to my husband, "*I really miss my ole' Kentucky home like I'm actually grieving it*" As I said the words out loud, my voice cracked, and you guessed it, the flood gates opened, and I found myself fully experiencing my 'ole Kentucky grief. The grief I had been pushing down.

As I felt my feelings, I understood what I was grieving fully. That little home, on that beautiful street in picturesque northern Kentucky, had been the place where I had first felt at home. When people have asked me where I'm from, I have been privileged to say that

I've lived all over this beautiful world of ours, but the cost was that I never really felt I had a home. When we moved into our sweet 1893 Italianate row house with the white picket gate, something magical happened to me. I felt as though I had roots; I had gained that feeling of home. I basked in that feeling for the entire eight years we resided there, and when it came time to move, even though there were countless rational reasons for it, from the exciting (new baby!) to the mundane (taxes), it did not matter. My home was in Kentucky, and leaving was painful to the point that I felt it in my bones.

Now, as a reminder, I moved six miles away. The best Mexican restaurant in the city is located there, as are the best places to buy bourbon. *I still go there often.* I think this is another reason I invalidated my grief; how could I grieve something still in my backyard? I don't know, but I did; I *really did.*

I was grieving what was and clearing it to make room for what would be. This type of grief often happens in our lives. Just because we think some transitions are less significant does not mean we don't have to grieve them. Honor these little griefs. They are just as important to cope effectively with as the big ones. Instead of judging them, let's appreciate them as opportunities to practice consciously coping with grief.

Structurally coping with trauma is a lot like grief. Healing through trauma takes time and intention, it also asks you to make meaning of the trauma and to integrate it into your life in such a way that you can accept it. All that being said, while grief is part of our developmental cycle, a predictable, inherently meaningful part of the natural world, trauma is random, chaotic, uncertain, unexpected, irrational. Trauma is its own beast for sure, but let's remind ourselves we can cope with our traumas. We can cope with tough things.

Before we dive in, let's take a moment to give some context to trauma. For this section, we are going to refer to both Big T traumas and little t traumas. Big T traumas refer to the big events that result in life changing outcomes, these are the usual suspects, war, abuse, assault, rape, car accidents, major medical events, major injuries, violence. Little t trauma refers to traumas that seem smaller, these are common day-to-day events which may not seem traumatic at first blush, but ultimately can cause significant distress and disruption. Job loss or unemployment, a death of a pet, a small injury, a recent unexpected diagnosis, a breakup, micro-aggressions or systemic disenfranchisement are all examples of little t trauma. Just like our smaller g grief, we are usually quick to invalidate the little t trauma when we experience it. We are also quick to invalidate other people's little t traumas. Give space for everyone's trauma, big or small, especially your own. Keep in mind, you cannot identify if someone else is or isn't traumatized, you may have a hunch, but ultimately you are not the decider of other people's traumas. Only they know what they experienced. They are the experts on them after all. We must acknowledge that there are some individuals who will misrepresent their emotional experience for secondary gains, but it is important to remember we can never really know their emotional experience and more importantly we must have compassion for them. If they are misrepresenting their trauma or emotional experience, they are coping ineffectively with something else.

I am certain all humans experience what we refer to as a small t trauma, but does everyone experience Big T Trauma? If so, is there a developmental purpose to Big T Trauma, similar to grief? I don't have the answers to these questions, but for me, it is the sheer presence of these questions that differentiates trauma from grief.

When I went in for my first session with my current therapist several years back, I arrived with my own case conceptualization in hand. Methodically, I spent most of our first hour listing out all the different mental health challenges I had faced. At one point, I nonchalantly blurted out "my father completed suicide about 15 years ago, and that was obviously traumatizing, but I've dealt with that, so I don't think we will need to spend much time on it."

Once I got through my 50-minute report of myself, I finally fell silent, waiting to hear her repeat back the diagnosis I had already given her and her thoughts regarding what we could do to address this mess that I secretly hoped she would tell me wasn't really a mess after all. Instead, calmly she just said to me "thank you for all that information; how are you feeling right now?"

I stared at her dumbfounded. This was the question I wasn't expecting. What does it matter? I thought. "I don't feel great", I stammered back.

"You don't feel great? So, what do you feel?" she challenged.

Dang. I squirmed as I let that settle. She had caught me in such a basic lack of emotional awareness it was embarrassing. I took a sharp breath in, and before I could think about it, I told her "I felt frozen in time. Unable to move, or feel, or…" I paused and felt my diaphragm tense *"…or breathe."*

As I spoke these things to her, I started to pay attention to the simmering emotional mess within me. I knew then that I had disengaged from myself, walking around like nothing was happening for months. I sat still and unmoving as my life burned around me, repeating to myself that everything was totally fine, nothing to see here.

As I walked out of my first session with her, it was clear that I had catch-up work to do with myself. I didn't realize it then, but that catch-up work was deeply related to the trauma from my father's suicide. It was also related to another more recent trauma I had experienced, one I hadn't even yet had the courage to name as a Trauma. But I trusted her, so I committed myself that day to facing this challenge and, by doing so, learn a better way to cope. I was tired of this cycle of ineffective coping leading to burnout; I was tired of feeling desperate. Desperation is an unsafe space for me, and I think for most of us. It can be coped with effectively, of course, but when you are desperate, you are more likely to do desperate things. We should work cooperatively to reduce desperate circumstances as a means of not only taking care of our neighbors but also caring for ourselves.

The Impacts of Pathology & Trauma on Reflection

Both pathology and trauma have impacts on our ability to reflect. Trauma is currently a very hot topic in the field of psychology. Trauma is a strange thing, and it can be difficult to define as you and I can experience the same event, and you may walk away a-OK, and I may walk away traumatized. Trauma is a personal thing. From the outside, you may look at me and think, "that weak person, I went through the exact same thing, and I'm okay. Why can't she just handle her crap and move on?" Because it doesn't work like that. We've just started to understand trauma, but we increasingly recognize its significance.

As I mentioned above, trauma is a very personal thing, and it can be hard to know if you have been traumatized if you don't have the verbiage to express it. I knew that something bad had happened to my family and me, but I didn't realize that I had been traumatized.

The symptoms of trauma vary from person to person, but here are some psychological and physical symptoms that may occur after someone has been traumatized: difficulty concentrating, confusion, anger, irritability, mood swings, anxiety, guilt, shame, withdrawal, social isolation, hopelessness, numbness, a disassociation between yourself and your body and/or your memories of the event, fuzziness regarding the time of the event (feeling very fast or very slow or both), difficulty recalling memories of an incidence, insomnia, nightmares, fatigue, easily being startled, racing heartbeat, panic attacks, chronic pain, weight loss or weight gain.

We need to remember that trauma changes the functioning of our brain. After being traumatized, our brain acts differently; this is particularly true if someone has experienced multiple traumas. Just like our beliefs about ourselves, which can be reinforced over time to become absolute truths in our minds, trauma over time reinforces to the brain that the world is not safe.

The brain is where we can better understand how trauma impacts us on a neurological level. While this is a complex process, I will do my best to give you a snapshot of how this works. Let's divide the brain into three key sections. In the first section, the lower back part of your brain is where your essential bodily functions and unconscious processes exist. This area of the brain is the most primitive. The middle part of our brain houses our sensory processes and our amygdala, where our emotions reside. This part of the brain is also where the function of the fight, flight, freeze , or fawn lives. Fight, flight, freeze, or fawn is our instinctual reaction when we encounter a threat. The upper part of our brain is where our executive functioning lies. It is basically the decision-making portion of the brain. It takes information from our senses, our past, and our knowledge about a potential threat to help us think through the best strategy. It takes a second for the information from the mid-point of your brain to reach the front part where your executive functioning lies. Over time, if an individual experiences consistent trauma, there is no time to let the threat be processed by the part of the brain that really has the complete picture of what is truly a threat and what is not.

One of my supervises worked with a child who was having a lot of anxiety at school and curiously would have behavioral meltdowns at school, but only on Wednesday mornings. We knew that the child had been referred after a significant fire had burned down their family home. We didn't know that the fire started in their toaster oven when they were making waffles one morning. It turns out the school served waffles on Wednesday morning, and it was a big deal. *Everyone* would get excited for Waffle Wednesday. It was the school meal highlight of the week, but once we knew about their history with waffles, their pattern of behaviors on Wednesday mornings started to make more sense. The child saw the waffles as unsafe, and their outbursts were as problematic as they were reflective of their ineffective coping pattern. It took a good amount of behavioral intervention with the child to help them relearn that the waffles themselves were not unsafe; they were just reflective of a traumatic experience they had had with them. Over time, the child recognized that when they saw a waffle at school, it didn't mean that they were unsafe and that the school would burn down; it just meant that it was Waffle Wednesday.

Similarly, pathology can distort your ability to reflect. That doesn't mean you can't reflect by any means; just pay attention to how these things manifest for you along the way of your conscious coping journey. A good example of how pathology can distort our perception comes from a client of mine, whose depression manifested as a dark, ominous cloud—a cloud so threatening that anything caught in its shadow shrunk. Because of this, the client struggled to see anything positive in anything. So, we had to practice together to identify the silver linings in these clouds. It was maddeningly uncomfortable for them and me, but the more we practiced, the more instinctual the behavior became. Once the skill started to feel a bit more accessible to them, we began to play a brilliant little card game called the game of gratitude. One day I pulled the hardest card. It asked simply, how can you express gratitude for crime? I sat stupefied and shrugged at my client. Without missing a beat, they confidently looked me in the eyes and said, "I can be grateful to crime because without crime, there would be no Dateline, and if there was no Dateline, I might not know who Lester Holt is, and I am definitely grateful to live in a world with Lester Holt."

Aha! The student had become the master! They had pulled out that silver lining without hesitation. They had developed a conscious coping strategy that addressed a specific need within their own pathology.

I stared at my client with tears of pride in my eyes and said, "For me, it is Josh Mankowitz, but I agree with your sentiment!" and we laughed.

You can't always stay in the dark.

During periods of trauma, acute pathology, or chronic stress, we may not have the capacity to process what is happening to us emotionally until things have simmered down a bit. This is a self-protection response that is encoded within us. The thing is that this is meant to be a short-term, not long-term, state. It is like our ability to manage stress, which we are wired to handle it in a short-term capacity but not to deal with long-term. We all have this skill, and we all do it from time to time. I know from experience that it is possible to do this for years on end, particularly if trauma gets invited to the party. I liken it to the voices of the adults on Charlie Brown. At first, you may be aware that you are not processing them, but over time, you start to just blank out to the sound, and it just becomes noise. The longer this goes on, the rawer it will be when you reengage. But you are strong, and you can cope with whatever you encounter.

Key Question: How do I feel about this challenge? What sense can I make of those feelings?

Ways to help cultivate the answers:

- If you have a problem identifying your feelings when dealing with BIG feelings, you need to make sure you are practicing with your little feelings. It is very difficult to learn to listen to yourself when you are in crisis; you must practice it during times of calm. Practice asking *how you are feeling* to yourself and genuinely respond. Do this three times a day: breakfast, lunch, dinner, or whatever makes sense. Do this regularly, and your ability to identify your feelings accurately and efficiently will increase. Bonus Points if you validate your feelings as well!

- Also, check out the MoodMeter (moodmeterapp.com) an app developed by Dr. Brackett and his colleagues at the Yale Center for Emotional Intelligence that will help you reflect and build your emotional intelligence (and your energy!)

- Play around with the visualization I presented earlier in the chapter. What works for you, what doesn't? Take it all or trash it all. Use it as a starting point and try to design a script or approach just for you.

· Track a pattern you would like to change. Don't work to change it right away; spend a week observing it. By investigating it, you will gain new perspectives on how to go about changing it. Please note this approach is only appropriate for small habits (i.e., your 7 am snooze habit, 3 pm sugar smash habit, or the 11:47 pm "Yes Netflix I'm still watching!" habit)— habits that are not immediately harmful to your health and well-being, or that of others.

CHAPTER 8

Absorb

> "Our old way of thinking–those problems are to be
> gotten rid of as soon as possible–overlooks the most
> important thing of all: that problems are a normal aspect
> of living and are basic to human creativity.
> This is true whether one is constructing things or
> reconstructing oneself. *Problems are the outward
> signs of unused inner possibilities.*"
> —ROLLO MAY

What feels like a million years ago, when one of my best friends and I were 20-somethings living the not-so-glam life of being young mid-westerners on the dating scene, we stumbled upon *a brilliant idea*. We were going to develop a luggage line inspired by the emotional baggage we had collected from some of our less-than-stellar dating experiences. There was the Barron, a large luxurious looking weekend tote that was unimpressive when you opened it up; the James, a deceptively small quick trip away bag especially convenient for trips involving infidelity; and my favorite, the mammoth-sized Joe trunk, perfect for sneaking around and moving across the country *without telling the girl you are dating* (true story!). Alas, we were never able to get our fantastic creations into production, yet I always smile when I remember them. Now, when I visualize what I need to put down, a fantastic piece of luggage frequently appears in my mind.

When we absorb, we find ways to integrate what we have learned to bring more value to our lives. We can absorb information primarily by practicing acceptance and meaning-making and, when appropriate taking action. In other words, we must find a way to unpack (action), re-purpose (meaning-making), or release (acceptance) that luggage.

Acceptance

When we learn to tolerate discomfort, we can start to accept uncomfortable and unacceptable truths. The best way I have found to practice the act of acceptance is to consciously *stop wishing* it were different, lean into what it is, allow what you think *could* or *should be* to melt away and start thinking about how this challenge brings value to your life. I have learned that I'm not effectively coping when I'm fighting an uncomfortable truth.

I can work to accept the unacceptable by practicing the act of acceptance. I've spent countless moments of my life lost in my toxic dance with myself. It was maddening to always be at war with myself. I was exhausting myself by fighting the imaginary enemy within, unable to see my patterns with any clarity. I have learned that it is hard to see patterns from the inside looking out.

There was, of course, no enemy, just a collection of learned behaviors that led me to a contentious relationship with myself. I waged war against myself. I perceived my challenges with my mental health as the ultimate mark of my defectiveness. If I could just stop being depressed, anxious, or furiously checking and rechecking the locks, then I would be a valuable person. My mental health was not the only battlefield—my body, family, trauma, and mistakes also provided useful fodder to bring myself down.

The cycle perpetuated itself constantly, in every domain of my life, for years, until one day, my therapist at the time said something to me that interrupted it. My therapist had challenged me to "make friends" with an aspect of myself I was not particularly fond of.

I was resistant, hemming and hawing, eventually saying something to the effect of "I've already accepted it, I don't think there is anything else to do about it."

"Have you accepted it?" they gently confronted me. "Accepting it means you didn't wish it were different."

Rats! They had read me so clearly. I realized that I had not accepted it. I mean, I said I did, but given how much I wished everything in my life was different at the time, it was all lip service.

I walked out of that session with a nagging feeling that we had uncovered something important, though I was not yet fully aware of what it meant. In the days that followed, I paid attention to what was happening inside of me, and I was amazed to witness how much of my energy was going towards wishing things were different. I wished I wasn't prone to periods of depression; I wished I wasn't disposed to a near chronic obsessive internal monologue that led me to catastrophize every little thing; I wish my father's suicide didn't happen.

I was wasting so much time and energy trying to change things outside of my control *that I lost sight of what I could control.* I could control my relationship with these things. I could learn to accept them. I could stop the cycle of wishing away what just is. I realized that I could reclaim all that wasted energy and learn different ways to cope.

I have the power to practice accepting unacceptable things for what they are. This does not mean I want these things; all it means is that I accept their inevitable presence and have learned I can cope with them by practicing the art of acceptance.

Meaning Making

Another aspect of absorbing is making meaning. Meaning-making is a tough one to explain. For me, it is a satisfying cognitive experience, like *ah! That makes sense!* When I make sense of change, chaos, and uncertainty, I experience a satisfying feeling in my hands, like the click you feel when you place a puzzle piece in the right spot. Sometimes it is accompanied by other circumstances-related feelings (happiness, excitement, overwhelm, even grief). Sometimes it happens quickly; often, it happens slowly over time, ever-evolving into deeper truths. Meaning-making is a process in which we are constantly engaged. When I make meaning of something, I have found a *conscious* place for it in my overall schema. I have found how the story fits into my larger experience. The story becomes part of my overall understanding, or schema, of my world, reality, and being.

I believe it is our job to find meaning in our lives. Meaning can always be found, even in the direst of circumstances. Once we have found that meaning, it is our job to learn from it and, when appropriate, share it with others as a means of supporting them in finding their own.

Opportunities to make meaning are endless. They are all around us, at every juncture and moment. But we must work for them; they usually are not served up to us. Meaning-making means looking at the landscape of your life and finding a way to make sense of your challenges within it. It is as if you are working on a giant landscape painting, Bob Ross style, of course, and slowly adding little things to it. Things that make sense to you, the artist and creator. They can make sense to others too, but they do not have to. Meaning-making is always worth the cost of admission.

I have a lot of baggage to unpack when it comes to the fourth of July. What was once an innocuous holiday has grown into something more substantial and significant in my life. It is a commingling of happy childhood memories and dark adult ones. It was bleak to have a festive holiday, a reminder of deep trauma and memories of what once was, looming on the calendar. A sad reminder of all that had transpired that fourth of July weekend in 2005, when my father chose to leave us.

But last year something amazing happened. I gave myself permission to make new good fourth of July memories. I remember staring down my neighbor's firework display from my backyard vantage point with my one-month-old baby on my hip. I was content. *This is good*, I thought to myself. In that moment, I reclaimed Independence Day.

I have learned that often we stand in our own ways when it comes to making personal progress in our relationship with ourselves. I had, after all, willfully stolen my permission to celebrate the fourth of July in perpetuity, just because it was associated with something else unpalatable. Do not get me wrong, for a few years, the day was a much-needed dedicated day of grief, but for the rest of my life? No, the cost of that is too great for me. I have learned that it is okay and necessary to move on from traumas and loss, not by denying them but by holding them near as part of your story. *You are more than just your traumas.* You have permission to move forward and fill the pages of the rest of your life with different stories.

If I am being honest, it was not just the fourth of July weekend I had hated for years; it started a month prior, a time of year I earnestly referred to as the "bad season" to my friends. Beginning with June 4th, my father's birthday, heading into Father's Day, and landing on July 6th when he died, that five-week period had caused me a great deal of angst. I would sense it looming in mid-May and find myself slowly digging out by the middle of July. It was a toxic pattern. Five weeks a year is a significant cost, and while my grief was earnest, it got to a point where I was no longer willing to pay that price. Also, as it is apt to do, life changed, and I had to make way for new things. Trans-formative new things.

Remember how I said that the "bad season" would always start on my father's birthday on June 4th? Well, June 4th took on a whole new wonderful meaning when we welcomed our first child. On what would have been my father's 70th birthday, his first grandchild was born. It gets even better. On June 1st of the following year, we welcomed baby #2. Now how is that for some grand meaning-making? What was once the bad season has been reimagined as birthday season. Instead of the "bad season," we now have "funfetti season."

I am happy to say that on the fourth of the year, it happened again, a full day of happy memories. As I've allowed myself to reimagine these days beyond my traumas, I've been able to add more comfortable data points to their historically uncomfortable emotional cache. This year we welcomed friends we had not been able to hug in two years. We rejoiced at the intimacy of having them in our home, and we reflected on what had been happening in our lives. *Embarrassingly, for us, that meant lots of talk about our love of Costco.* At the end of the day, watching fireworks together as a family unit made it clear this is the *new* pattern now; my relationship with the fourth of July has officially shifted. As I watched the fireworks, I saw them in a light, a celebration of the reclamation of my life beyond trauma. The fireworks reflect my liberation.

Take Action

Sometimes to cope effectively, we need to act. In life, most of what we cope with day-to-day is less acute than the examples we have explored in this book. Quite simply, our mental health gets bumps and bruises. Remember, just because you can't see a psychic injury doesn't mean it isn't there. Sometimes conscious coping requires grand approaches, but most commonly, it requires the equivalent of a band-aid.

In practice, what this looks like is a brief check-in to triage as needed, and if it can be addressed at the moment, great! That means we were able to cope efficiently, which is something we only get limited control over, so it's not a metric to judge ourselves on. However, we should take a moment to express our gratitude and appreciate the extra energy we saved. When we experience a coping challenge, the simplest answer is often the right one: we need to engage in a self-soothing behavior. There are many types of self-soothing, or coping skills, as we will refer to them. I think pretty much any behavior can be a coping skill, depending on the person, their tolerance, and the context in which it is utilized. If it is appropriate and safe for the individual to engage in and they get energy from it, it doesn't hurt others and it doesn't get in the way of them coping consciously, I would classify it as a healthy coping skill. Keep in mind that in the context of coping, where everything is ever-changing, a coping skill may be healthy in one situation and less healthy in another.

Practically, this is what this could look like. You could have a glass of wine after work. Because you drink responsibly and it doesn't disrupt your other self-care activities, like taking Fido for a walk, it is probably a reasonably healthy coping skill for you to utilize. Now, if something changed and all of a sudden you started daydreaming about that glass of wine at lunch, and then when you go home that glass turns into a bottle, and because you are wine drunk, you shrug off taking Fido for his walks, and because you are drunk, you sleep terribly and wake up raw and cranky the next day, and the pattern continues, then voila! Now we have transformed that healthy in moderation glass of wine into an unhealthy coping skill.

Here is the deal: in an example as extreme as this, it may be possible for someone external to notice something is up, but for the most part, we are the only ones who have access to the data of how we are coping—*that is why it is so important to pay attention!* The example above was based on an experience of a client of mine. The transition of this pattern happened after they experienced significant trauma and grief. It was no wonder they attempted to cope by numbing out. It was the path of least resistance and the only path that provided total (temporary) relief from the immense pain they were grappling with. I have great compassion for that. In that great gulf of the challenge, I get how their humanness took over and helped them cope in the most fundamental way it could. But somewhere in the midst of this, my client woke up. They said it was intense, *like a flash of lightning in a pitch-black cellar.* When they saw the depth of the situation before them, they knew they must stop drinking.

And they did. I will always be ever inspired by their insight, resilience, and courage at that moment. They stopped drinking and, for about a year, focused on dealing with their grief sober because the act of doing so was the ultimate show of love and devotion for that which they had lost.

And here is the most impactful part of the story: they are back to enjoying their craft beers. IPAs, in particular, bring them great joy. They enjoy learning about them, comparing them, and, yes, reasonably enjoying one at the end of the day. They consciously coped by knowing that drinking was not a healthy coping skill to use during emotionally intense times. The temporary numbness that drinking affords is too tempting for them. Still, to this day, there are days and times when they intentionally abstain from alcohol, but for the most part, their relationship with alcohol as a coping skill is back to being healthy.

It is important to note that coping skills exist on a spectrum. They can be over-utilized just as much as they can be under-utilized. For example, I can have a glass of wine after work, and usually, that is a healthy choice for my stress management, while alcohol of any quantity is unhealthy for others. If you pay attention and listen to yourself, you will know what is healthy vs. unhealthy for you. If you judge yourself for using a certain skill, be interested in why you feel that way. Judgment takes energy from you. The goal is to refuel and reclaim your energy, so if you are judging yourself, we have a leaky pipe, and we always want to be curious about leaky pipes.

Also, please do your best to resist the urge to compare yourself to others. I used to tell clients who told me that cleaning was part of their innate self-care that I was jealous. It was kind of a silly thing to say, primarily because I was modeling for them my judgment of myself. Also, it distracted both parties from the fact that everyone has their way of taking care of themselves, and judging our way of doing so against someone else's is meaningless as well as a waste of energy. Again, we encounter the recurring theme that you alone are the one who is best equipped to judge what works and does not work for you. Make sure you give yourself the permission and flexibility to allow things that previously served you to no longer serve you and vice versa.

Most importantly, this is a space to have some fun! Often there are fun and playful ways we can practice coping skills. Unfortunately, we have demonized the idea of fun and play for adults. By thinking these things are for children only, we have lost sight of the vital role that fun and play have in our self-care and how we learn about ourselves and our greater world. You need only to be around children for a brief period to connect with how important fun and play are to their bio-psycho-social development. Adults are no different.

One of my favorite assessment questions to ask clients is, "What do you do for fun?" Only about 40% of the time do people have a quick answer for me. Often people look at me dumbfounded and frustrated that they cannot answer this simple question. This is a good example of how divorced we have become from the importance of fun and play in our lives. It is another area where our cultural mores have informed an unhealthy and unrealistic approach to taking care of ourselves by suggesting that engagement in fun and play is a meaningless, frivolous pursuit for adults. Fun and play have many benefits to our mental health and ability to cope; making room for fun and play is an important part of how you consciously cope. The first step to prioritizing these things is permitting yourself to do so. So have some dang fun with it! Try some new coping skills on for size. We always want to be building our tool kit, and I don't know anyone who doesn't like a shiny new tool. Here is a list of 101 coping skills for you to play around with. Also, keep in mind that any of these, when integrated into your routine, can become part of your self-care.

1. Have a picnic
2. Color in a coloring book
3. Read an internet comic
4. Listen to a podcast
5. Do a puzzle
6. Breathe deeply
7. Do a mindfulness activity
8. Make a vision board
9. Dance (like nobody's watching)
10. Take a bath or shower
11. Watch an educational talk
12. Look at the stars or clouds
13. Plan a getaway or something else to look forward to
14. Compliment yourself
15. Eat healthfully
16. Go for a walk
17. Sweat hard
18. Stretch
19. Take a nap
20. Sit and rest
21. Meditate
22. Drink water or tea
23. Turn off your phone
24. Put on some lotion
25. Wash your face
26. Get a haircut, or a massage, or a manicure, or a pedicure, or just make it a whole dang spa day
27. Go style your outfit of the day
28. Give yourself a pep talk
29. Remember, and if you are comfortable doing so, talk to someone you have lost
30. Say yes to something outside your comfort zone
31. Say no (yes, saying no is self-care)
32. Buy yourself a treat
33. Clean your space
34. Declutter your space
35. Let in some fresh air
36. Forgive yourself
37. Forgive others
38. Create something
39. Play a game
40. Journal
41. Sing out loud
42. Spend time outside
43. Stay hydrated
44. Change your sheets
45. Listen to music

46. Play music
47. Hug someone
48. Hug your pet
49. Phone a friend
50. Light candles
51. Diffuse essential oils
52. Practice gratitude
53. Set goals
54. Learn something new
55. Ask for help
56. Join communities
57. Participate in hobbies
58. Tell your story
59. Make a list
60. Lean into your support system
61. Go swimming
62. Laugh
63. Read a book
64. Watch a movie
65. Do yoga
66. Play
67. Take a digital detox
68. Declutter your mind
69. Take a day trip
70. Cook or bake for fun
71. Go to a party
72. Go on a nature hike
73. Garden
74. Volunteer
75. Call a loved one
76. Go to a museum
77. Play a sport
78. Learn something new about your family
79. Recite positive affirmations
80. Watch the sunrise or sunset
81. Take a sauna
82. Try a new food
83. Go to the zoo
84. Get lost
85. Find your new favorite comedian
86. Get a mentor
87. Give some else a gift
88. Challenge negative thinking
89. Schedule "unscheduled" time
90. Write a letter to a loved one
91. Write a letter to yourself
92. Slow down!
93. Cuddle

94. Apply a facemask

95. Take a road trip

96. Buy yourself flowers

97. Practice good boundaries

98. Go bird watching

99. Create a new routine

100. Make amends

101. Embrace yourself (do it for real, give yourself a hug, there is no one more deserving of a hug from you)

For the remainder of this section, we'll dive a bit deeper into specific categories of coping skills or actions you can take. Keep in mind that as long as it doesn't hurt your or anyone else, and you use it intentionally, pretty much anything can be an effective coping skill.

Altruism

Altruism is a great but often overlooked coping skill. By helping others, we increase our own sense of belonging and connection. Belonging and connection are always meaningful to our mental health. Additionally, altruism feels good because it stimulates dopamine, oxytocin, and serotonin, all of which are neurotransmitters that can help us cope more effectively with stress. There are many different ways you can volunteer your time and energy. Often just a few hours helping others or your community can provide you with great quantitative and qualitative benefits.

As a bonus, altruism usually crosses over with other coping skills. When you volunteer, it can act as a catalyst for further social engagement. If you are struggling to connect and build community, altruism is a wonderful place for you to start. A shared vision creates an accessible way to build trust and rapport with others. Altruism often involves some level of moving your body or engaging your creative mind, both of which are known to trigger those feel-good neurochemicals as well.

Asking for Help

To ask for help, we must first be vulnerable. By allowing ourselves to be vulnerable and admitting that we cannot do everything by ourselves and without the help of others, we allow ourselves access to a greater tool kit. When it comes to our mental health, our internal struggles are often not apparent to those in our external world the way a broken leg would be. One of the best things we can do for our mental health is to ask for help, which is a great show of vulnerability.

Often, we worry about how others may view us when we ask for help. Still, if we take a step back and normalize that we all must ask for help occasionally, we can stop judging ourselves for engaging in a behavior that helps to support our mental health. It may seem like a small thing, but it is not. I reflect upon the loss of my father and the fact that he didn't ask for help during his greatest time of need. I would have done anything to help him, without pause or judgment, even if that would just be to say "I love you and I want you here with us regardless of what mistakes you may have made." I often reflect on this tragic missed opportunity within my family unit. I'm of the sound opinion that asking for help is one of the most powerful things we can do. I'm especially impressed by my clients; I am so proud of them for taking the first step and admitting that they need help.

If you are in a state of crisis and need help there is immediate mental health support you can access, all you need to do is reach out. If you are in the US you can call the national crisis hotline at **1-800-273-8255,** or if you prefer visit the national crisis chat here: **suicidepreventionlifeline.org/chat/**

Many municipalities also have local support available, both at home and abroad. This is where google is your friend, just type in "mental health crisis help" and your zip or post code. You can also find a list of crisis phone numbers from the good folks at Find a helpline here: **findahelpline.com**

You can also call a friend or family member who you can be vulnerable with. Tell them honestly what is happening to you and then *let them help.* We often think people won't help us when we are in crisis. **Give them the benefit of the doubt and ask them**. If neither of these options fit, you can call 911 (or your local emergency dispatch), or to the nearest ER. Even though it will take time to work through a mental health crisis there is immediate support available to you if you ask for it. Remember that you can cope with tough things and the moment you reach out for help is the moment you start coping more effectively with your crisis.

Assertive Communication

For whatever reason, most of us have learned to communicate by dancing around what we really think, feel, want, and need. Part of this is politeness, I am sure, but the other, more insidious part is that we have received messages about how being bold and direct is wrong. The truth is that I do not believe in mind readers, and if there are no mind readers in life, then we all must do our best to communicate what is happening within us as openly and directly as possible. Assertive communication is not the same as aggressive communication, just as it is not the same as passive communication. Assertive communication is the ability to express all your ideas (not just positive or negative ones) in a confident, controlled, calm, and clear manner. Assertive communication helps you effectively communicate your needs and expectations.

Asserting or maintaining your boundaries often requires assertive communication. Remember, you must speak your boundaries.
I know it is scary and uncomfortable, especially if you aren't used
to doing so. Often, we are nervous or scared for what the other
person will say or do when we put our boundaries out there, which
is a valid fear. Often people don't respond well if we tell them about
our boundaries afterward, effectively changing the rules of engagement mid-game, which is okay and to be expected. However, the
unconformable truth is that people like boundaries. They help us
by supporting realistic expectations, and usually, over time, people
warm to them. In other words, be like the lifeguard; whistle down
violations immediately and assertively.

The goal of assertive communication is to respect yourself as
much as you respect the party with whom you are communicating.
Assertive communication is a skill, and it can take a lot of practice
to feel confident using it, especially if it is a new tool for you, but it
makes such a difference in how you take care of your mental health.
A great person to practice assertive communication with is your
therapist; if you can do it with us, you know you can do it with others.

Creativity

There is significant research to support the effectiveness of creativity in both the treatment and prevention of mental health disorders.[8]
The act of being creative and allowing your brain the space, time,
and energy to do so is an important coping skill. When we engage

---

8   J. Leckey, "The Therapeutic Effectiveness of Creative Activities on
Mental Well-Being: A Systematic Review of the Literature," *Journal of
Psychiatric and Mental Health Nursing* 18, no. 6 (February 17, 2011): 501–9,
https://doi.org/10.1111/j.1365-2850.2011.01693.x.

in creative activities, we use different parts of our brain, which is particularly helpful when we are trying to keep our emotive vs. our rational brain in the driver's seat.

Creativity often gets overlooked because we are focused on the outcome of creative engagement. If you are going to spend three days working on a painting, what value will that painting have for you when you are finished? Will you be able to sell it for money? Will you be able to proudly display it in your entry and have people compliment and validate your talent? Could you spend three days working on the painting without any need for any additional outcome, except for your sole enjoyment of doing so?

We often view creativity as creating art, but creativity comes in many different packages. What feels creative to you and sparks that part of your mind is unique to you. Celebrate whatever that is. Let yourself play and explore. You may find yourself engaging in a passion you did not know existed before trying it out.

Forgiveness

Forgiveness is tough. First off, we often think of it as something we do for others, but that is not the whole story. Forgiveness is not *for* someone else; it is *for* you. It is about saying I have carried this anger, hurt, irritation for long enough, and I am ready to release it. Sometimes we are not ready to forgive, but usually, the main thing that holds us back from forgiveness is not knowing how.

I am sure this will sound familiar, but how you forgive is up to you. Some people find the tools for forgiveness within their spiritual belief system; others find it helpful to engage in tangible practices such as writing it down and throwing it away. Still others need to verbalize their forgiveness. Although I have used these tools, I tend to visualize what I need to forgive and find a place outside of myself to place it. I have a metal lawn flamingo in my backyard near my psychological junkyard. When I struggle to forgive something, I hand it over to Frankie, my forgiveness flamingo, and it helps. I give it over to him, and I can put it down.

Gratitude

Research shows us that gratitude is where the seeds of happiness are sown.[9] Of course, we should express our gratitude for each breath we breathe, but we are often swept up in just surviving with all the challenges, changes, chaos, and uncertainty we face. We forget to connect with the beautiful, mystical moment of now.

Just as there is an infinite number of things to be crotchety about, there is an infinite number of things to be grateful for. One takes energy from you, and one gives energy to you. Which ones would you prefer to spend your energy mining? A great way to cultivate more gratitude in your life is to take some time each day and practice. Complete a grounding activity like the one we reviewed in the previous chapter. When you are done, list three specific, unique things you are grateful for. Here is my list from this morning.

1. Crisp winter mornings
2. Comfy pants
3. The Bengals (my hometown team!) are going to the Super Bowl!

It seems like a small thing, and it is, but don't underestimate the power of this small thing. It should be noted that if you think it is

---

9   Charlotte van Oyen Witvliet et al., "Gratitude Predicts Hope and Happiness: A Two-Study Assessment of Traits and States," *The Journal of Positive Psychology* 14, no. 3 (January 15, 2018): 271–82, https://doi.org/10.108 0/17439760.2018.1424924.

useless or a waste of time, it won't work. So, if that is the case, find a different way to engage your sense of gratitude in life. The goal is to reflect on your gratitude more often instead of just stumbling into it now and again.

Interrupt Your Patterns

Once you have learned your patterns, it is time to interrupt them. The only way to change them is to interrupt them; otherwise, they will continue perpetually. I know it can be scary to interrupt these patterns, but facing uncomfortable things is how we grow. Remember, you can cope with tough things. Or, as my therapist has said to me, you can continue to dance the way you always have, or you can change your dance steps.

The good news is that you can interrupt your patterns in small ways and big ways. The small ways in practice may look like taking a mindful breath when you notice the pattern presenting itself, standing up and stretching, taking a drink of water, discussing it in therapy, hot or cold showers or hand washing (temperature change interrupts our automatic nervous system if we are dysregulated), or even avoiding the pattern altogether. Of course, avoiding is rarely the answer, but as we will discuss shortly, intentional avoidance can, on occasion, be the correct way to interrupt a pattern.

On occasion, we need a reset in life. There are two types of resets: soft resets and hard resets. A soft reset is needed when you find it hard to catch up with your coping. A soft reset may look like taking a mental health day, going for a long hike, a social media detox, or even just having a scheduled "unscheduled" day. A soft reset requires at least eight hours (preferably 12) hours and should be focused on delivering a large intentional dose of self-care. It can be one or many forms of self-care, as long as you do it intentionally and in such a way that you are taking care of your health. If not done right, a soft reset can shift into a day of avoidance, which has a high cost. We need a soft reset from time to time to help us catch up and regroup.

We need a hard reset when we have developed patterns in our behaviors, relationships, and environments that prevent us from coping effectively. If you need a hard reset, you need at least 48 hours to reset. Ideally, you will have a full week. *I know, I know* that feels gratuitous, and truly it is. It is extravagant to give yourself a week to focus only on your care for yourself, but that doesn't negate that that may be what you need to do to care for yourself the way you need.

I believe that a hard reset works best when you change your scenery. If you can spin it, go to a hotel or a town a few towns over. Visit a friend, or even stay in a different part of your house. If the only change in scenery you can realistically access is building a pillow fort in your living room and staying there for a bit, then do that. Hard resets require that you disengage from your patterns. Create some space between them and yourself, and brainstorm ways to enact meaningful and immediate change in how you are coping. That may mean something drastic, like quitting your job. If that is the case, take a deep breath, and make a realistic plan about how you can do so. If you need to wait six months until you complete the portfolio project you are working on so you can get the new job you want, that is fine, but realistically how are you going to take care of yourself so that you can do so without sacrificing your health and wellbeing over the next six months? Do you think the best plan is to march in there on Monday and dramatically resign? If it is some- thing you really need to do, then okay, but how will you cope with the potential consequences of doing so? Are there things you need to salvage, or is the healthiest choice really for you to burn that bridge down and never look back? I don't know the answers to these questions, but you do. You need only to do the work to find them.

I want to say one more thing about resets: I believe that they work best when you can slow down and experience quiet. This may just be me, but I have a hunch this is true for most of us. I have learned that clarity presents most when I have slowed down. I must be still with myself to really hear myself. A good way to gauge your ability to sit with yourself is to put your phone down and just be for 15 whole minutes. Don't do anything else, no TV, no music, no books, no technology. Don't even meditate. Just sit and be. What happened when you did so? What clarity did you gain?

Patterns thrive when we are so busy that we don't have clarity on what we want or need, our boundaries and expectations, or how we self-sabotage. So, if you can, even if you aren't burned out, find the time to take yourself out for a reset in the near future. All it needs to be is a mega dose of self-care, and I can't wait to see what a good reset looks like for you!

Journaling

The act of getting things down and expressing them is always a solid coping bet. Journaling has the bonus of helping you process what you are experiencing in a unique way. It is a physical expression of what is within you that taps a different part of your brain, automatically giving you a unique lens to view through what you are experiencing. Research has shown a link between journaling and positive behavior change.[10]

---

10 William Miller, "Interactive Journaling as a Clinical Tool," *Journal of Mental Health Counseling* 36, no. 1 (January 1, 2014): 31–42, https://doi.org/10.17744/mehc.36.1.0k5v52l12540w218.

One of my clients found a new strategy for journaling that I think is quite fantastic! They were having difficulty separating their work and home life and had been struggling with the fact that journaling (a long-term coping skill of theirs that had been particularly useful) was becoming stressful, and they were avoiding it. They realized they had been avoiding it because they usually journaled when they got home from work, but doing so just kept them thinking about work, and they were resentful that work had taken over their journal entries. So, they got a new journal specifically to journal at work. Now they wrap up their day by journaling what they need to capture at work and do their personal journaling at home at 9 pm. This client reported that keeping these things separate has been very beneficial to their stress levels. *Way to consciously cope!*

Let Things Go

We had to clean out our garage unexpectedly recently. We had amassed a pile of boxes from our pandemic delivery reliance, and as a brutal storm clipped through our valley, water got in the garage. *Voila, soggy boxes!* We did not realize the accumulation of water in the garage because the storm happened at night. Truthfully, we were too enamored by the accompanying stunning lightning storm to care much about the garage at the time.

As annoying as it was to have to clean the garage unexpectedly, I have to say that I find something therapeutic about projects like these. The power to purge stuff, reorganize your space, and reclaim something from chaos is my go-to when I need to feel some sense of accomplishment. I have not always been this way, but a few years back, I was inspired by Marie Kondo's Netflix special. When I watched it, it was not the transformation of the spaces that took my breath away (although those were quite spectacular in their own right), but the transformation of the people's emotional state and relationships. I was so inspired by her special that I committed to doing a full, top-to-bottom KonMari on our home. It took three months to complete, but the act of doing so was truly life-changing (she does not lie). I have learned to accept that part of how I can gauge my mental health is by the state of my environment. I have learned that chaos in my environment triggers my anxiety, leading to overwhelm and apathy. I have learned to respond with action when I feel uncomfortable in my space.

The entire process of deep cleaning a space reminds me of therapy. If we are going to do a proper deep clean, we should do it all the way. When we do it all the way, we pull everything out, put it under the light, categorize it and assess whether we still need it or not, and then finally pack it in a way that makes sense. It is the same when we unpack something emotional: all of it must be examined, cared for, categorized, and then consciously and thoughtfully released or packed away in a better, healthier, more compassionate way. The hardest part of this process is not to give up halfway through when the mess you made doing a proper cleanup is somehow larger and more overwhelming than it had been when you first got started. I have learned that when tackling difficult things, it will often get worse before it gets better. I have learned that I can persevere through difficult things.

When I started to pay attention to my energy investments, I was surprised at how many things took energy from me that I did not question or adjust to fit my needs better. One of the best examples of this is external to me: my chaotic collection of things. Yes, literal stuff. Stuff takes energy from us, and the more stuff we have, the more energy gets sucked up by it.

The most poignant example of this was an Isabella Fiore black canvas makeup bag. Sounds innocuous, right? Well, you would not know it, but this makeup bag brought up bad memories, uneasy feelings, and regrets anytime I looked at it. I purchased this makeup bag three days before my father's suicide, at the Saks in downtown Chicago, just because I could. I am not sure even how much I ever liked it. Rather, it was an example of the wanton consumerism I was engaging in during that time. Resistant to seeing my own privilege, I remember calling my father and demanding that I be allowed to buy this thing. I remember his voice in that call; he had become increasingly resigned over the previous few months, and with a tired disregard, he told me to "just get whatever you need." I remember hanging up the phone and, in a cringe moment of entitlement, I announced loudly to my friend and the rest of Saks "he is so annoying! I don't know why I have to ask for money, he has enough to let me get what I want." I think back on this memory with sadness and disgust for myself. The purchase of this bag was one of the last memories I have of what my life looked like before everything imploded. I see myself as the example of who I never want to be again: entitled, dismissive, and superficial. Quite frankly, all I can do is hold my breath and cringe when I think about it. While I am grateful that I have this yucky benchmark to help define who I aspire to be now, I still struggle to engage this memory without getting sucked into the sheer yuckiness of it all.

Every time I saw that makeup bag, every piece of this yuckiness came slamming back onto me. Even worse, even though I was not really using the makeup bag, I had kept it prominently placed in all five of the apartments I had occupied since my father's death. I mean, what the hell was that about?! That was the question that came to mind as I picked it up to assess whether it gave me joy. It was immediately clear: not only did this object not bring me joy, but it also brought me shocking waves of shame and sadness. I do not remember ever having a positive emotional response to seeing it.

As I thanked the bag and packed it to take to Goodwill, something amazing happened. Instantaneously, I felt a weight lift from me. It was a beautiful bag, and I hope it will bring someone else joy, but for me, the joy was in releasing it, letting it leave my psyche because I no longer needed that daily reminder of shame. Now when I think about that makeup bag, I feel joy, mainly because after all that time, the makeup bag finally taught me a healthy lesson—that our emotional connection to *stuff* is real, and we need to question it.

Make Amends and Identify Restorative Action

We all make mistakes. We all have times when we must make amends and seek restorative action. You are not blameless, neither are your parents or neighbors; none of us are. We have arrived at another uncomfortable truth. It is very seldom in life that something is 100% one person's fault (although these things happen, especially in cases where people are victimized by others); most of the time, there is shared "blame" in any conflict. It may be that I have 99% of the responsibility, and you have 1%. Still, it is shared. We both have work to do. That being said, I think we need to be insightful into differences, especially extreme differences in responsibility in any given situation. Suppose I had 99% of the responsibility. In that case, I believe I must seek out the opportunity to make amends with you and collaboratively find a way towards restorative action. I should bear the majority of the burden in doing so.

I should note that while it is important to make amends, there are times when making amends with others would cause them more harm. In these cases, it is appropriate not to make formal amends to the party but instead perform some ceremony to demonstrate and release the regret. As long as you take meaningful action towards making amends, you can complete this task even if you cannot do so with the other person.

Meaningful Action

Sometimes meaning-making requires action. As I mentioned above, sometimes, we have to create our own ways to make meaning. Recently a client told me they planned to walk 593 miles over the next year and track their progress with their Fitbit. I was impressed and applauded them just for their desire to tackle such a goal, but then they told me why they had chosen that number. That was the number of miles back to the spot of their sexual assault several years prior. An assault that had left them traumatized and disempowered AND an assault that has progressed their personal growth and demonstrated their strength and resilience. They planned to make meaning with those miles, track that journey back to the place where it happened, and reclaim that part of them. I am always so impressed with the creative, meaningful ways people show up for themselves when they are consciously coping.

Medication

Usually when we think about a quick fix solution for our mental health challenges the magic pill is medication. One pill will turn it all around! This is an oversimplified approach; medication isn't a fix. Instead think of it as a tool. An imperfect tool, one that takes refining and one that many of us may need to utilize across our lifespans.

Perhaps instead you find yourself on the other side of this pendulum. You are resistant to medication worrying that medication may change you too much, making you "not like yourself". I get it, that is where I was for a long time. Even when I was in grad school studying to be a psychotherapist, I was still resistant to meds. I feared that they would change who I was, make me less funny, more stale – a husk of myself. I didn't like being anxious or depressed, but the thought of losing my razzle dazzle didn't feel like a fair price to pay just to "feel better". Fast forward to me now, this morning I got up and took my two meds. When I go to bed tonight, I will once again take my two meds. I have come to understand that for me, I have a chemical imbalance, one that requires ongoing medication as an intervention. Once in grad school we made genogram of our family's mental health history. I didn't need to go much beyond my father to see that chemical imbalances run in our family, but when I did so, I saw how significant it was and I started to understand this part of myself differently. These two meds haven't changed me (I hope you can still see my razzle dazzle in these pages), but what they have done is incrementally bumped me up. I still have symptoms and struggles, but I don't spin out like I once did, lying in bed for days on end as the scene around me deteriorated.

Think about medication like this, we all have canoes going down the stream of life. Some people are born with two paddles, some with one, and some with none. Those of us who have chemical imbalances may be lacking a paddle or two and need a permanent replacement. For others sometimes the stream can swallow up one of your paddles, or break it, and you need time to replace or heal it, and so medication can act as a replacement paddle. My medication has been part of how I consciously cope. It is not the only tool I use though, in fact the research shows that it is a combination of medications, therapy, and mental health hygiene has the best outcomes for those of use that have chemical imbalances.[11]

Medication is not for everyone, and not everyone has to take it forever, but it is a tool to help us consciously cope if we need it. I trust your judgement on this one, you are after all the expert on you, but I hope you give yourself permission to entertain this option if deep down you think it might help. One last thing I would like to say about medication, is that it can take time to find the correct combination of medications and dosages. Don't give up. Find a prescribing provider you can talk to honestly about what is working and what isn't working with your meds, and then give yourself and your body time to find the right fit.

Meditation

Meditation is not about turning off your thoughts; it is about learning to focus your mind. As we have discussed, many things in our world can distract us from what we desire to consciously focus on. Focus is an important skill, and focusing your mind (especially during periods of stress and overwhelm) can help you stay on your path to taking care of yourself. Meditation, and the associated practice of mindfulness, have been shown to have positive effects on mental health in the short and long term.

Meditation is not a quick fix. It is a skill, and I advise that you approach it as such. You will not be able to access the great benefits of a meditation practice if you only reach for it in crisis. You must practice this skill during moments of stasis and emotional regulation to

---

11   Pim Cuijpers et al., "Adding Psychotherapy to Antidepressant Medication in Depression and Anxiety Disorders: A Meta-Analysis," *World Psychiatry : Official Journal of the World Psychiatric Association (WPA)* 13, no. 1 (February 2014): 56–67, https://doi.org/10.1002/wps.20089.

utilize it effectively when you are feeling unbalanced or dysregulated. Many programs will support you in developing a meditation practice, but you will need to commit yourself to practice regularly. Many of these programs are free or low-cost, and you can start with just five minutes a day. You do not have to become a meditation master going on full-day meditation retreats to reap the benefits of meditation.

Movement

The relationship between exercise and mental health is well-documented; making healthy choices for your physical health translates into very real benefits for your mental health as well.[12] However, this is often an area where we engage in extremes that can be unhealthy. We go all-in with exercise, usually in January of each year. We throw all our energy behind it and head in with unrealistic expectations. Typically, we burn ourselves out and end up exhausted and unable to engage this tool healthily or at all. This is one of the major reasons I titled this section "movement." We do not have to do P90x every day of the week to take care of our mental health; instead, we can just go for a ten-minute walk around the block. Yes, it can be that simple. If that is what feels accessible to you, then that is what you should do for yourself. Whether it be a simple yoga routine, a personal dance party, or a HIIT workout, just do what feels right for you. Moving helps us to process emotions and express them proactively.

The more I have paid attention to my mental health, the more I have learned to listen to what my body needs. A few months ago, on a typically gray winter day, I found myself feeling increasingly

---

12   William P. Morgan and Stephen E. Goldston, *Exercise and Mental Health* (Taylor & Francis, 2013).

unsettled and distressed. Every time I stumbled upon these feelings, I would also think I am feeling depleted; I need to go for a walk. I heard myself, but I didn't listen because going for a walk didn't feel like a priority to me. Finally, one day, in tears and confused as to why, I heard myself say it again, and this time I listened. It was 15 degrees outside, my walk lasted all of ten minutes, but being in the presence of nature in the brisk winter air served me well. The benefits were stunning. I was affirmed that I had done what my body needed me to do. It needed to move, and when I did so, the *stuckness* associated with my feelings of distress was released. Of course, I needed to address more things underneath this, but the immediate release was an important reminder that our bodies know what we need. They communicate it, but we must listen to it, even when it feels inconvenient.

Music

Music is magical. Music helps us understand our experiences in a unique way. We can use music to evoke certain emotions and states. Music is unique in that creating and consuming music are both incredible coping skills. Both have been shown to reduce anxiety and depressive symptoms in adolescents and adults.[13] Like other creative interventions, music allows for a different part of your brain to work, explore, and process. Although I don't use music as part of my emotional process, I know many people who do so effectively. One of my clients found great solace playing in a jazz group on the weekends; they told me they found comfort in having a few hours

13   Norma Daykin et al., "What Works for Wellbeing? A Systematic Review of Wellbeing Outcomes for Music and Singing in Adults," *Perspectives in Public Health* 138, no. 1 (November 13, 2017): 39–46, https://doi.org/10.1177/1757913917740391.

a week just to get lost in the music. They also mentioned that the music's improvisational style helped them gain more confidence in their ability to improvise in their day-to-day life. *Snaps all around!* Another fantastic example of conscious coping.

I like to keep a coping playlist close by so it's easy to reach on tough days. "Shake it Off" by Florence and the Machine, "Don't Stop Believing" by Fleetwood Mac (the entire album *Rumors* is another excellent example of meaning-making), "Roll with the Changes" by REO Speedwagon (obviously), "Gotta Be" by Desiree, "Hold On" by Wilson Phillips, and "Let Them Say" by Lizzo are all mixed together and guaranteed to help me get out of the funk and onto the fun. These songs are curated by me and help ground me in my ability to cope with tough things. I've been developing this playlist for myself for several years now, and it is so lovely for it to be immediately available to me. I bet this is also something nice you could do for yourself, too. What are your coping anthems?

Nature

We are starting to learn what eastern cultures have long embraced: that nature and spending time within it is a crucial way we take care of ourselves and our mental health. We can find one of the more interesting examples of this wisdom in the Japanese concept of forest bathing. Forest bathing is the simple act of spending time with nature, consciously connecting with nature free from the distractions of modern life.

Although this concept has been present for a long time in eastern cultures, it has only recently become popular in western culture. Still, the evidence is already being presented regarding how beneficial this practice can be. Researchers found that forest bathing provided immediate short-term benefits to individuals' mental health. Researchers were able to see significant shifts, particularly in anxious symptoms[14]. Our modern world does not necessarily lend itself to making our engagement with nature a priority, but when we do so, the benefits are almost immediate. It can literally (and figuratively) be a breath of fresh air. Finding a special time, place, or way to engage in nature is not only part of how we connect with ourselves but also our greater world.

Pets

Kitty cats, dogs, turtles, or any type of pet can positively impact your coping. There is a ton of research to demonstrate the healing power of pets.[15] During the pandemic, the impact of pets on our mental health was studied in a different way. Most of us experienced a new degree of social isolation, and our pets played a meaningful role in keeping us connected. Even if you cannot have a pet, vicarious engagement with animals can be meaningful. I mean, hello, do you think all the cat videos on the internet didn't have a fundamental purpose? Even better, go volunteer at a local animal shelter. They always need help, and you can get a double-dip of coping by combining your love of pets with some altruism.

Reading

A funny thing happens when you finish school. You may have your degree, but there is a good chance you have lost the love of reading

---

14   Kotera, Richardson, and Sheffield, "Effects of Shinrin-Yoku (Forest Bathing) and Nature Therapy on Mental Health: A Systematic Review and Meta-Analysis," *International Journal of Mental Health and Addiction*, July 28, 2020, 1–25, https://doi.org/10.1007/s11469-020-00363-4.

15   Odean Cusack, *Pets and Mental Health* (Routledge, 2014).

you had when you were a kid. It does not happen for everyone, but for many of us, the educational system makes us practice the act of reading for a conscious and structured purpose. With the continued focus on reading as an academic skill, we lose our love for reading just for fun. Graduate school particularly has that effect on people. I found myself unable to crack a book for pleasure for five years post-graduation, and ultimately when I did, I found myself pulled to professionally focused books. The idea of reading fiction felt wrong and uncomfortable; if I were not learning something, what would be the point? Reading is an often-overlooked coping skill and has been shown to positively affect our mental health, including reducing depressive symptoms, building empathy, and improving cognitive functioning.

One of my clients is a voracious reader and makes it through nearly a book a week, all because they have to find quiet to read, and making time for solitude and space helps them keep their self-care rhythm. To them, reading is the linchpin that holds their entire coping game in place.

Fascinatingly, when I challenged myself to pick up a novel a few months ago, I found out that I enjoyed it. I enjoyed it so much that I read another, and then another after that, but then something stressful happened, and I stopped reading. It felt like the energy I needed to read was the energy I could not spare, but I realized my mental health was negatively impacted when I stopped. Since then, I have been tracking my engagement with reading, and I have found something intriguing: I usually feel better, less stressed, more able to cope, and have more energy when I am reading regularly. When was the last time you picked up a book? When can you pick up a book next? What type of book are you going to pick up?

Sex

Sex is one of our more primal coping skills. Many of us are encoded with the desire to make our bodies, and the bodies of others, *feel good*. Historically we have shamed sex and sexuality, and thus again, we arrive at another uncomfortable truth. There are things, such as sex, that, if dealt with in a heartless or unintentional manner, can become something you have to cope with instead of something that helps you cope. Permit yourself to use sex and your sexuality as means to play, have fun, and effectively manage your stress levels.

For some, sex may not be on the coping menu. Not to worry, just like anything else on this list, partake if you want, pass if you prefer. Sex is another example of a coping skill that needs to be moderated for you, by you. Wherever you land on the spectrum, permit yourself to use sex (or sensuality) as a means to cope. Just remember the golden rule: as long as it doesn't hurt yourself or others, it is fair game.

Social Engagement AND Solitude

Being with people, sharing in the communion of the here and now, can be hugely helpful. To me, the feeling of belonging is the good stuff. *We need each other*, but we don't need each other all the time. We all have learned this in a different, very authentic way during the pandemic. We knew we needed each other in our rational minds, but after all this time without each other, we now know that we need each other for emotional health and wellbeing. We now know we need each other in a new way. Connecting with other humans heals us and helps us commune in our coping.

Remember earlier in the book when we explored how different people have different cognitive processes? Another example of this is how introverts and extroverts approach this type of action differently. People on the extroverted end of the spectrum tend to get energy from social engagements, while introverts tend to expend energy. This does not mean that introverts do not like social engagements; it just means that they can feel depleted and, on occasion, leave the party a little early. There are many metrics to gauge your introversion vs. extroversion, but here is my favorite way of assessing for introversion. When you go to a party, do you prefer to drive yourself? If the answer is yes, you are most likely an introvert because when an introvert is done, *they are done.* For me, it can be literal agony to be stuck someplace after my energy is depleted; as such, introverts tend to like having their own ride home.

The other side of social engagement is our need to spend time in solitude with ourselves. While this may be a more natural and energy-giving activity for an introvert versus an extrovert, it is still important for extroverts. Solitude allows us to practice connecting and listening to ourselves, and in a world so full of distractions, this is a skill that we need to hone. Even if you find solitude to not be as fulfilling as time with others, it is still important to take time alone. If you struggle to spend time alone with yourself, you may be running from or avoiding some aspect of yourself that makes you uneasy. This is a yellow flag; be curious about this. You do not need to go full hermit and spend gobs of time with just yourself, but regularly scheduled me time is an important part of how you take care of your mental health.

Therapy

Therapy is a tool. I take great pleasure in the normalizing impact it has when I tell clients about my own usage of therapy. It shows that even if you are a professional in this space, you still struggle and benefit from therapy. Therapy gives you a safe space to process and learn, and when you find your right fit therapist, you also get a trusted collaborator.

As I continued my work with my current therapist, I had a sudden realization. I had erroneously thought that if I were hilarious enough about it, I could sidestep my trauma.

It did not work.

The suicide of my father was not the only trauma I have experienced. Immediately after his death, a cascading series of events transpired. In one week, my family went from comfortable and seemingly financially secure to destitute. My father was a folk hero in my family, he was the one who got a job as a paperboy at the tender age of 10 to start saving to go to college. He was the one who became an executive and still made it home on the 5:15 train for dinner. He was the one who would always give generously to everyone around him. He was successful, he had made it, and we had the material things to show for it. *Or so we thought.* When my mother went to the bank the day after his death there was $347.59 in their joint account, and not much else. In short order our home was foreclosed upon. I couch surfed a bit trying desperately to find a way to afford to stay in college. Fortunately, I was able to stay in school; unfortunately, I was able to do so due to predatory student loan lenders ensuring the consequences of this decision would remain with me for years. *We make the best decisions we can with the information we have at the time.* I am grateful I was able to stay in school, AND I am still angry that I had to make financial decisions under duress when I was particularly vulnerable.

My life became a very real game of survival. I was privileged in many ways, too many to count, actually—I was able to study abroad, get my degree, and land a job out of college. I was, however, in a constant state of financial uncertainty and chronic stress, one that would extend for years. As I dug myself out of it in my late twenties,

I promised myself that I would do my best not to put myself back in the same place where I felt so insecure. It is awful to feel that way, and if you never have, please know that having financial security is a significant privilege in life. Be extra gentle and compassionate to those who are struggling. It is a pain you cannot imagine unless you have been there.

The thing about it was that once I finally made it to a point where I no longer felt financially desperate, I was in my early thirties, and I decided to take the road less traveled. To quit my full-time, sure thing, job (with benefits!) and start my own business. I am not sure I understood that part of the gamble with opening a business is putting yourself in a financially insecure place. At first, I was like, this is fine, I can deal with this discomfort, which transitioned to, this is getting stressful and overwhelming, which then morphed into, what have you done, you messed everything up! And then I just got disengaged and stopped paying attention.

During one session, as I was slowly unraveling this knot, I said to my therapist, "I just feel like the bottom is going to fall out!"

"You keep saying that," she reflected; "what do you mean by that?"

At this moment, I experienced one of the strongest, strangest things I have ever experienced. A moment that helped me relearn the power and the purpose behind therapy. She was correct; I kept saying that phrase. But, I was not sure what it meant? When I asked myself at that moment, I immediately felt a whoosh in my stomach like I was falling. It was the sensation of when you are on top of the roller coaster, and you start to fall, your stomach creeps upwards, and doom sets in.

As I felt myself fall, I was no longer in her office. It was a beautiful day, the first sight of spring. Chilly but warm enough to justify sitting outside and indulging in a nice glass of white wine. My husband and I had just sat down when suddenly the radio changed to commercials. *I hate commercials on the radio*, so I popped up to change the station to something else. As I walked across the deck, I stepped exactly right on a board that had become soft due to the spring rain. Without a moment to process it, I was falling. The fall was slow yet fast (a hallmark sign of trauma). As I hit the deck, I was sure I had broken my leg. I hung there for a moment before my husband could get to me. Finally, he hoisted me out, and immediately I felt the discomfort of my body going into shock. I was nauseous and disoriented, not to mention in a tremendous amount of pain. Nothing appeared broken, but I was unable to walk. A trip to the ER confirmed that I had jacked myself up about as much as possible without breaking anything.

I was on crutches for about six weeks after the incident, and it took me about 12 full weeks to physically recover. During this time, I started to do something funny. Well, actually, it was not funny, even though I convinced myself it was. I made a joke out of the whole experience. I had deck trauma, I would tell people jovially. I now have deck-phobia, I would chirp to anyone who would listen. It was all such a *hilarious* joke.

Except it was not.

About a month after the incident, we decided to have the deck removed, which was a positive that came out of this whole thing. My husband and I had walked out on the deck briefly to consult on how we wanted to proceed with this project. Immediately, I felt the panic well up in my body. It bloomed into a full-blown panic attack, and my husband had to escort me off the deck. After that incident, I had *actual* evidence to support that this had been a traumatic experience for me, but I still did not take it seriously.

I had other pieces of data to support how impactful this experience had been, as well. At the zoo, one of my favorite places in the world, I looked down and noticed that I was standing on a deck. Without a thought, I bolted to the nearest pavement I could find. My smartwatch alerted me to a spike in my heart rate and reminded me to breathe. Huh, that is interesting, I thought to myself. I proceeded with my day without a second thought. I was resistant to seeing the present trauma in front of me; it was part of the knot of emotions I had been ignoring.

As I felt myself falling in my therapist's office, I blurted out, "The deck!"

"The deck? What about the deck?" She leaned in closer and I noticed how my body had shifted into stiff terror.

"I'm falling, always falling, always afraid of falling." I faltered. "I feel so unsafe all the time...all the time my body is falling, and I cannot catch myself." I started to shake as I felt myself fall.

Somehow the trauma of my financial insecurity after my father's death, triggered by me starting my own business and the trauma of falling through the deck, had crossed over, sending my brain a constant overwhelming message of impending peril and doom. I realized that the vibrating sense of doom that I had been feeling for the last six months was the sensation of me falling *over and over and over again*. It was as if I was constantly watching a looped video in the background. I was dizzy with clarity; my body had been scream-ing at me for months, trying to communicate how unsafe it felt, how traumatized it was from the experience of falling.

It was not a joke. It was *trauma*.

"Your safe; you are here now." I heard her voice cut through the past and bring me back to the present. *I was safe*, I heard myself reflect. I sat securely on her couch, grounded in the present moment.

"I was traumatized by my fall through the deck; it wasn't a joke. It was real," I processed out loud.

"Yes," she validated me. I acknowledged the feelings of fear and overwhelm, and just like that, the sense of falling began to ease.

This experience is my favorite story to tell about therapy, primarily because it demonstrates the power of therapy. I needed that information reflected back to me before I saw it for what it was. It was such a joke bouncing around inside of me, such a joke I just blew off all the many signs that showed it was not a joke. When I sat in the trust and compassion in that space, and she helped me unpack what had happened, a rush of energy surged through my body. It is impossible to explain exactly, but it was as if I got that proverbial monkey off my back (or in this case my brain).

Somehow my brain had transposed my trauma, and that simmering I told you about that I recognized at our first session? That simmering was my body falling over and over and over, in a state of unchecked, unrelenting anxiety. This is why I had disengaged. *It was so much*, I thought incorrectly that I could not cope with it. Instead, I had avoided what it was, and my brain coped automatically, and unsurprisingly, ineffectively. I was so scared of the instability; it kept me in a space of hyperarousal and hypervigilance, looking for the next plank to fall. My brain was screaming at me to keep it safe, and I just dipped.

But, as you know, we can't just avoid things forever. This conversation with my therapist was the first step towards healing all those unresolved pains and anxieties I had been running from, it was therapy that helped me to find my direction towards coping effectively with them.

Treat Yo' Self (or Indulgence)

Now let us have some real talk about everyone's favorite type of self-care, *indulgence*. It is okay to indulge; you should live your life enjoying the things you enjoy. Whether your pampering consists of a pedicure or massage, a piece of decadent chocolate cake, a shopping spree, or a brand-new video game, it does not matter. It is fair game if it brings you joy, and it is not an everyday thing.

Just remember that indulgence usually comes with a cost, and that cost often is higher than other types of coping skills. As such, pampering yourself is usually not an everyday occurrence. Further, it is important to remember that if you just reach for this skill, it will not be that helpful. In fact, I often think when we overindulge, we get indulgence fatigue or a feeling of exhaustion from indulgence and desire to return to some level of moderation.

Typically, this happens to me in early January, after the traditional six-week holiday binge of food, drinks, celebration, family, events, gifts, and frenetic energy between Thanksgiving and New Year's. I think a lot of us feel this way, which is why we crave that reset of January. Treating yourself is absolutely part of how you take care of yourself, but remember, as tempting as it is, it is not the only way—even if it is usually the most fun!

Taking Some Time and Space (or Intentional Avoidance)

Sometimes you need to press pause. On occasion, intentional avoidance is an appropriate tactic. *I know, I know.* I have spent this entire book saying that avoidance is a *no-no*, and it is, most of the time. Just not all the time.

A few years back, I was chosen to attend a leadership program. While I was there, we took an assessment to determine our conflict style. Well, I took that test and sat there overconfident amongst my peers, for I had scored very high on compromise as my conflict style. I was certain that my strategy of compromise all the time was the correct one. I peeked over my colleague's shoulder next to me and judged their high avoidance score. It turns out I was totally wrong; the whole reason we did that assessment was to demonstrate that we need to use all the different tools, not just one. Avoidance is one of them, at the right time and place. Avoidance had a purpose. It was a novel thought for me. Since then, I have intentionally allowed for avoidance when it is appropriate to do so.

Practically this can look like waiting to make a big decision until all the information comes in, taking time and space from a relationship to assess and formulate what you need to say to heal or progress or end that relationship, or, when you are in a true survival situation, expending your energy on only survival. Just remember that eventually, you will have to come back from that place. The longer you stay, the more likely you will lose time due to being chronically disengaged from your life.

The key difference between regular avoidance and intentional avoidance does not include denial. Intentional avoidance acknowledges the concern and makes tentative plans on when you will return and resolve this issue so that it doesn't become unfinished business. You expend energy when you avoid things. Think of it as a makeup bag full of feels floating around in your psyche. It takes energy to keep it there, so you should use this tool with extreme moderation.

I have learned that challenges are best dealt with at the moment they present, but I know that is a luxury that isn't always available to me. In other words, I have high expectations AND realistic expectations for how I cope. I have learned to accept that avoidance of challenges comes with significant cost, which is usually not worth it. I keep all this in mind when I choose to use intentional avoidance. I am also realistic with myself about the cost of doing this. All I'm doing is kicking the can down the road. Eventually, I will need to deal with it. Avoidance is not always the wrong strategy; sometimes, the best approach is intentional inaction. However, it should be used sparingly. Avoidance is the high-interest credit card of coping skills. *Be mindful when you use it.*

Magic Wand

Yes, I know. I spent the whole book talking about how there were no quick fixes or silver bullets, and now I'm showing up with a magic wand, but hear me out. The magic wand is not a quick-fix; it is just a magic question. It helps you visualize what needs to happen next. If you are stumped and don't know what action to take but have a nagging feeling you need to do something, the magic wand is the tool for you.

Simply ask yourself this: what would change if I had a magic wand and could make all this better?

Abracadabra! Reflect upon your answer and keep yourself open for opportunities to cope with this challenge in unique and meaningful ways.

This works because it forces you to imagine what things need to change to get you closer to what you want and need. I have a dear client, who once a session never fails to tell me that if they could just win the lottery, they would quit their job, and they would be happy. When we dissect this vision for their future together, we always seem to land at the same conclusion. Even if the client won the lottery, they would still go to work because they would be bored. The difference is that they would go to work at a different job, a job that was more fulfilling, a job they didn't feel stuck at. Sure, it had great benefits, fairly good pay, and a little bit of flexibility. It wasn't a bad job; it just wasn't a life-giving job. My client was struggling with the cost-benefit of this tension. Were they willing to sacrifice meaningful work for the benefit of a comfortable life? Perhaps the opposite was true; they needed to find a new job that gave them life and deal with the financial consequences. Neither is a "wrong" choice, but the cost-benefit became more apparent when we took finances out of it. After six months of us reviewing the magic wand question, one day, the client shifted. Instead of saying "I need to win the lottery," when I asked them what they needed to do for themselves, they said, "I need to get a new job," and a few months later, *they did.*

Keep Exploring

You must remain open to finding new, healthy behaviors to engage in. By keeping a curious attitude, you allow yourself to keep learning all the nuances of what serves you best. As a reminder, what serves you now may not always serve you or may not be something that serves anyone else. Allow yourself to stay curious, try new things, and learn about all the diverse ways to care for your mental health.

Who knows, you may find that listening to podcasts, making pottery, or Irish dancing will be your coping skill. Or you will become a potato chip connoisseur or Rubix cube enthusiast. The sky is the limit. Give yourself permission to fly free and learn to cope the fun way.

Key Question: What do I need to do to consciously cope with this challenge?

Ways to help cultivate the answers:

- First, determine if you need to take action, make meaning, or practice acceptance. Or do you need to do some combination, or maybe even all three? If you can determine the category of what you need, you can start refining what you can do for yourself.

- If you get totally stuck, ask a friend what they would do. Worst case scenario, you can engage socially and authentically with someone else, potentially learning something new.

CHAPTER 9

Capture

> "Let go of who you think you should be,
> and embrace who you are."
> —BRENÉ BROWN

Now that we have ditched the one-size fits all options and you have started doing all this hard work to learn about your mental health and how you cope, how are you going to document it? Part of the journey of EMBRACE is to find ways to memorialize what you have learned about yourself outside of yourself. So, what do you think? How can you best remember the lessons you've learned from conscious coping?

Use Your Senses

Every once in a while, when I am on an airplane or in a hotel, I get a delightful surprise in the bathroom: they have my special memory soap. When I was in fifth grade, we moved from Chicago to Hong Kong. Twice a year, we would travel home to see family. On these long international journeys, I would dread going to the bathroom. I still do as an adult; I really must be in a crisis to use a plane bathroom. I am terrified when the bottom of the toilet flops open, and it makes that awful, strong sucking sound. *I just hate it.* I remember, though, as much as I hated the bathroom, I loved the soap. It was this exact soap, a smell of deep almond, gardenia, and some other mystery smell I have never quite been able to put my finger on. This soap calmed me at the end of my scary bathroom trips. It soothes me now, connecting me to what was and what is.

On occasion in my adult life, I stumble upon the memory soap, and I immediately feel its uplifting nature. I love it. It is a pleasant surprise anytime I encounter it. I do think I have been running across it more in the last few years. One day I will be brave enough to ask someone what it is and then fill my home with it. For now, I continue to love the glimpses of meaning and joy it gives me.

All our senses are deeply connected with our memories, but our sense of smell has the closest path to our memory. For this reason, scent can be utilized as a therapeutic tool. Scent has been shown to help reduce anxiety and increase feelings of happiness.[16] This is what this soap does for me. This scent reminds me of those wonderful times when the airplane toilet was scary, but my family and I were living an adventure. We were bonded together, the four of us. I miss these days with my family. These days highlight the beauty of what we had. I hold these memories with honor; they deserve as much spotlight as the darkest ones. Catching the smell of this scent on occasion helps me capture that lesson and hold it nearby.

---

16   Masahiro Matsunaga et al., "Brain–Immune Interaction Accompanying Odor-Evoked Autobiographic Memory," *PLoS ONE* 8, no. 8 (August 20, 2013): e72523, https://doi.org/10.1371/journal.pone.0072523.

Tell Your Story

One of the powers of therapy is sharing your story with someone else. The ultimate shame-buster is to share your story continuously and courageously. Just make sure you give others the same opportunity and value their experience as equal to your own. Sometimes we share our story with one or only a handful of people, but sometimes we desire more. We want to share on a broader scale about our journeys, the challenges we have faced, and the lessons we have learned. I get it; after all, that is part of my journey with this book. To share the good news that we all need to know: that we can cope with tough things.

So, if you want to write a book, make a film, or even do a TEDx talk, *do it*. Share your journey. Help people find time and space to invest in their journeys. Be compassionate with yourself and others. Lean into the challenges our mental health brings us and embrace the opportunities that come with them. And most importantly, celebrate everyone's progress *because it is progress*.

Celebrate

We need to make celebrating more of a priority! We put off celebrating too much. It is foolish to deny ourselves the privilege of celebrating a job well done.

Your resilience deserves to be celebrated! Find a meaningful way to call out yourself and your awesomeness. Sometimes celebrations are planned, sometimes they are spontaneous, but never miss an opportunity to celebrate your strength and resilience. I've been lucky enough to be privy to some of my client's celebrations over the years. Some of my favorites include:

1. Going to Disneyland without the kids and living your best big kid life
2. Buying yourself a beautiful piece of jewelry just to show yourself you care
3. Getting a tattoo to capture AND celebrate the meaning you have made
4. Having a boudoir photography session for your own personal pleasure
5. Indulging in a glass of 20-year Pappy Van Winkle

Try not to put off celebrating. My business grew to the point where we could open our fancy new office space in December 2019. It was so nuts, and honestly expensive, that I just decided we would celebrate the office in a year in December 2020. It made so much sense! We will just wait to celebrate; I'm so smart! I thought to myself. Well, you know how this story ends. In March 2020, the pandemic hit, and boom, our beautiful, fancy, new office was shut down. In the months since everything has changed, our needs have also changed, and eventually, we will maybe get the opportunity to celebrate moving out of our office. Still, we will never get that chance back—to celebrate what was a freaking HUGE accomplishment at the time. My office key captures the memory of this lesson. I use it so rarely now that I instantly remember this lesson when I lay eyes upon it. Never miss out on celebrating your progress in life. If it feels significant to you, share it with others, make it a thing, and treat it like a flipping priority. You deserve to celebrate *all* the things.

Key Question: What lesson does this challenge teach me? How can I capture these lessons to remind me of what I have learned from this challenge?

Ways to help cultivate the answers:

- What memories does this challenge invoke for you?

- How do you visualize this challenge as a tangible object? What does that object reveal to you about the challenge?

- If your best friend or significant other or family were to give you the best surprise gift ever, what would it be? How could you give yourself at least a small aspect of that in the near term?

CHAPTER 10

Endure

"So live as if you were living already for the
second time and as if you had acted the first time
as wrongly as you are about to act now!"
—VIKTOR E. FRANKL

It takes time to cope effectively with most of life's great challenges, but if we continue to cope with life's small challenges in the midst of grappling with the great ones, we are progressing towards healing. *We are progressing towards triumph.* I once had a therapist who told me that if I didn't feel up to learning a lesson from the universe this go around, not to worry because the lesson would come back around. I sat in awe. I instinctively knew it was true, AND it was absurd. Now, several years on from that conversation, I see it happen all the time. I do not think there is any significant meaning to it (in that I don't believe some entity is making these things "happen for a reason"). Instead, I think this happens because we all have so much to work on and many different ways to do so. In other words, your growth potential is endless and ongoing. We all have our work. In the last five years, my work has been to find a way to take care of my mental health. And I did it. Thank goodness I did because the universe has kept up its end of the bargain and offered me up some primo challenges (hello, having two babies in a pandemic!).

It was just over two years after my initial session with my current therapist when I said something that I was not sure I would ever be able to say.

"I feel healthy mentally and emotionally," I said hesitantly, "which is weird."

We sat in silence for a moment before I continued. "It feels like I am finally free just to notice my feelings, allow them to be, and not be so caught up in reacting to them. It is not like I am not feeling; I am. It is just so different than it was. My mental health feels so much more manageable and overall takes up so much less space in my life. It is like I have learned to engage with it in a way that means I have to work at it every day, but because I work at it every day, it is not easy, but it is easier."

"Like you can step back and see the whole picture?" she suggested.

"Yes." I allowed myself to continue to process out loud. "I guess I feel grounded and capable of coping and taking care of my mental health because I am paying attention and engaging in it. I trust that I can deal with the issues on the horizon, but I don't have to be consumed by them, especially not before I reach them. I also do not have the heaviness of the past weighing me down. I feel as though I have finally caught up. I do not have a backlog. I am just present to right now."

"You feel mindfully present," she stated.

"Is that what it is?" I wondered out loud.

"It sounds like it," she continued. "I am hearing you say that you have found a way to take care of your mental health by allowing your emotions to be, to notice them, be curious about them..."

"And take proactive action when I need to, versus just reacting to them," I added.

"How do you feel right now?" she inquired.

Tears suddenly sprang up in the corners of my eyes; the words came without much thought. "I feel grateful and proud, really grateful and proud."

This is what I had been working on for the past few years—catching myself back up to the now and allowing my mental health to be a valuable, meaningful *part* of my life. This is the skill; this is the outcome this book seeks to help you obtain—a new way of being with yourself that will positively ripple through the landscape of your own life. Since then, I am proud to say even with all the challenges I have faced, I am still engaged. I still consciously cope. I have embraced myself in a better, more effective, more efficient, more fun way.

At this session with my therapist, the full scope of work ahead came into focus. This is ongoing work. It does not end, or at least I don't want it to end. It is important, and as I started to share these pieces with my clients, I realized I had stumbled upon something quite significant: the more confidence we have in our ability to cope, the more our resiliency builds. The more our resiliency builds, the more we grow our confidence in our ability to cope. This is why it is so important to do the work.

It seems so small to write it down. Yet, these small words belie the ample space this truth takes in my life. We talk a lot about uncomfortable truths, but here is a comfortable one. If you stay engaged, you can cope with whatever you face. You have control over it, and you can do it. *I know you can.*

I know deep within you; *you know that you can too.*

I practiced the art of conscious coping. You can too, and I sincerely hope you will join me on the journey to coping effectively. Remember, we call it a journey because it is ongoing. The beauty is not in just the destination but in the act of walking it. Your job is to maintain the discipline to continue to do the hard work of conscious coping.

We forget that discipline is love. Discipline is not punishment; discipline is a committed expectation. Having a structure is a gift. It helps support us to cope. It is why it is so important that we discipline our children with love. You need the discipline to endure this ongoing work, discipline for the work, and the constant tough looks at yourself. Discipline to get back on the coping horse when you fall off because when it comes to conscious coping, falling off the horse is not the problem; getting back on is.

I used to imagine that good mental health was like riding a slow horse on an uncomplicated trail. As I wrote this section, I pictured a person riding a horse on a smooth, open trail into the sunset, a serene look on their face. It seemed so nice, so picturesque, so easy, and as I sat envisioning that scene, trying to unpack what it meant to me, I started feeling phony, like I was only telling part of the story.

After sitting with it for a moment, I realized that was what I wanted my mental health to look like. Smooth, picturesque, relaxing. And it is okay that that is what I wanted it to look like. That is what many of us want, but I do not think that is the reality. In fact, this unrealistic expectation for ourselves and our mental health can be quite damaging.

I feel a bit anxious but more empowered by owning that my mental health is not really like that. So, I went back to the drawing board, thought about it some more, and realized that while riding the horse is part of it, it is not all of it. In fact, riding the horse is a highlight, but not the most important part. When we ride the horse and get lost in that beautiful moment of rhythm and flow, we do not think about all the different moving pieces that go into it; we just are. We can exist there in the pureness of the moment. There is beauty there; it may just be a glimpse of beauty, but it is beauty, nonetheless. I had to look beyond the serene image to see the complete picture because the initial picture I chose was what I thought things *should* look like. Easy, but that is not the reality. Reality requires a fuller picture.

When I was eight years old, my cousin had horses. I loved to ride her horses. My parents invested in horseback riding lessons for me, and for a period in my young life, it became quite a passion of mine. One day we were out on the trail, transitioning into a full gallop as the sun beamed on my skin and the pure summer air wrapped its breeze around me, and I felt the freedom of being at one with the triumph of that moment. Then suddenly, it was over, and I was on the ground, stunned, confused, scared, and banged up. I still, to this day, do not fully remember what happened. Still, we pieced together that my cousin's GAP sweatshirt had come untied and flew in the face of my horse, spooking him and throwing me off.

Physically I was okay given the circumstances. However, the emotional sting of that moment impacted me way more than any physical injury I had. For the first time, I was confronted with the reality that something that brought me so much joy could potentially be so dangerous. *So uncertain.*

I immediately refused to get back on the horse. I ended up walking behind my cousin, lead in hand, the rest of the way back to the barn, anxious to tell my parents what had happened. Once they were assured I was okay, my parents became insistent that I get back on that horse. And I was insistent that *I was not* going to get back on that horse. And so, a war of will broke out until my parents bribed me to get me back on the horse. I forget what they bribed me with, but whatever it was, it must have been great because I remember being very nervous and salty as I pulled my sore body back into the horse's saddle.

I got back on the horse. I rode it around, just a little bit in the pasture. As quickly as I was on, I felt reconnected to what I loved about riding the horse, even though that connection now included the knowledge of what *I did not* love about riding the horse.

The process of conscious coping is like riding and inevitably falling off a horse. For a long time, I used to beat myself up for falling off the horse of mental health. I couldn't understand why I could not just get my crap together enough to ride serenely through the even trailhead, gently moving through life with comfort and ease. While there are certain things and patterns that I engaged in that did not move me towards that goal, the ultimate problem with that goal is how unrealistic it was. What matters when it comes to our mental health is that we know that falling off the horse, and getting back on, is the only way we continue to get glimpses of that serenity.

And so, we close this journey and ride off into our versions of the sunset. I want to express gratitude to you for walking the journey towards conscious coping and allowing me to be part of it. I am sending support to you as you continue your journey beyond this book. Always remember, you can cope *effectively* with tough things. *We all can.*

Key Question: How can I use the experience of this challenge to help support me in doing the ongoing work required for conscious coping?

Ways to help cultivate the answers:

- What did this experience teach me about conscious coping?

- What energized me from this experience? What can I use to propel myself forwards?

ABOUT THE AUTHOR

Laurie Sharp-Page is an author, entrepreneur, and psychotherapist who is passionate about teaching people how to cope more effectively with life's varied challenges. She loves to find innovative and fun ways to learn more about our mental health and how we cope with it.

As a practicing existentialist she spends her days attempting to cultivate calm in her multi-generational household, while embracing the chaos of it and finding meaning within it. In her spare time Laurie likes to bake bread, watch bravo, and drink rare bourbons.

To get more conscious coping resources, tools and fun, join the Conscious Coping Club at www.ConsciousCoping.Club